# Multinational Banks
## Their Identities and Determinants

# Research in Business Economics and Public Policy, No. 8

## Fred Bateman, Series Editor

Chairman and Professor
Business Economics and Public Policy
Indiana University

## Other Titles in This Series

# Multinational Banks
## Their Identities and Determinants

by
Kang Rae Cho
Assistant Professor of
International Business
Pennsylvania State University

UMI RESEARCH PRESS
Ann Arbor, Michigan

Produced and distributed by
UMI Research Press
an imprint of
University Microfilms International
A Xerox Information Resources Company
Ann Arbor, Michigan 48106


Library of Congress Cataloging in Publication Data

**Cho, Kang Rae, 1947-**
  Multinational banks.

  (Research in business economics and public policy ; no. 8)
  Revision of thesis—University of Washington, 1983.
  Bibliography: p.
  Includes index.
  1. Banks and banking, International.  I. Title.
II. Series: Research in business economics and public policy (Ann Arbor,
Mich.) no. 8.
HG3881.C553  1985      322.1'5          85-1123
ISBN 0-8357-1668-6 (alk. paper)

*To My Family*

# Contents

# List of Tables

# 1

# Introduction

No post-World War II business development has had a greater impact on world economic, social, and political order than the expansion of multinational corporations (MNCs). The tremendous growth of MNCs in the postwar period attests to the vigor of this organizational form. Sources of MNC growth in manufacturing and extractive industries, MNC contribution to enhanced world economic efficiency, and MNC behavior with respect to competitors, customers, and the governments of host and home countries have been the focus of considerable research over the past twenty years, and a fair consensus on these now seems to have been reached.

The world has witnessed increased adoption of the multinational form by the nonindustrial sectors as well—most notably the financial sector. Although existing data do not allow an accurate comparison, the scale of multinationalization in the financial sector seems to be as impressive as that in the manufacturing and extractive sectors. A major category of multinational venture in the financial sector is the commercial bank, particularly U.S. commercial banks that, for various reasons, have felt the need to establish a presence in foreign markets. As of the end of 1975, assets of foreign branches of U.S. banks were at $176.5 billion, up from $3.5 billion in 1960. They reached $476.5 billion by the end of 1983. Growth of the foreign banking business of U.S. banks has been far greater than growth of the domestic business. Paralleling this growth is the increase in the number of overseas branches from 131 in 1960 to 900 in 1982. Similar growth trends can be observed among commercial banks of other developed countries and recently, even a few developing countries have seen the multinationalization of their commercial banks.

Despite such impressive multinational growth in the banking sector, and although the development of new international financial markets (such as Eurocurrency markets) has been extensively investigated, there have been few studies on the multinationalization of commercial banks. It is the intent of this study to provide a comprehensive examination of the growth of multinationalization in the commercial banking industry by studying the scope and nature of commercial banks' multinational operations and deducing determining factors of their growth under different market conditions. A theoretical model will be developed to explain multinational banks (MNBs), and will be used to explain important factors contributing to their growth in foreign markets.

The definition of a multinational bank is subject to a variety of interpretations, and the term is frequently used interchangeably with such other terms as international bank and transnational bank. Broadly, multinational bank can mean any banking institution that engages in cross-border banking transactions whether it be by correspondent relationships, direct lendings to foreigners from home offices, or direct investment abroad. In many instances, however, multinational bank is used to refer to a bank with a physical presence outside its home country through a branch, an agency, a wholly owned or a majority owned subsidiary, or a bank formed by a merger of two or more banks based in different countries. Some authors further qualify their definitions in terms of the number of countries in which an MNB owns banking offices, the number of banking offices that it operates outside its home country, or the forms of its overseas representation. Wellons (1976) defines an MNB as a deposit-taking institution operating in more than five countries through branches or subsidiaries. Brimmer (1975) regards an MNB as a bank with three or more branches outside its home country. Robinson (1972) maintains that only branch representation can serve the aims of an MNB.

In this study multinational bank is defined as a banking institution:

1. whose major functions in a home country include deposit taking, extension of credits, and provision of related banking services; and

2. that has established institutional presence in the form of branches in one or more foreign countries to engage mainly in the provision of such banking services.

Excluded from this study, therefore, are noncommercial banking institutions and commercial banking institutions that engage in transborder banking operations through institutional means other than branches.

In an attempt to develop an integrated approach to explain the phenomenon of multinationalization in the banking industry and to uncover the determinants of MNB growth, the study will focus on the following questions:

1. What advantages does a bank need to allow it to compete against local and/or other foreign banks in foreign host markets?

Why is foreign rather than domestic operation advantageous in serving foreign markets? and

Why does a bank choose to exploit these advantages itself rather than selling or licensing them to local and/or other foreign banks?

2. What are major considerations of MNB management in deciding the expansion of multinational involvement?

These questions will be addressed through a descriptive analysis of the scope and nature of MNB operations, development of a theoretical model and its empirical test, and an investigation of actual MNB activities in foreign markets.

This study is organized into seven chapters. Following this introduction, the scope and nature of multinational banking operations and the patterns of growth of MNBs will be investigated in chapter 2. An overview of theoretical developments in multinational banking and MNBs will be presented in chapter 3. That chapter will provide an understanding of the current stage of research on MNBs and present the need for an integrated approach to explain them properly. Chapter 4 will concentrate on developing the integrated model to answer the questions raised in this study. Chapter 5 will give empirical results of the application of the model. Chapter 6 will explore the activities of the dominant group of MNBs, U.S. commercial banks, in two different settings in the Asia Pacific region—offshore banking markets (such as Singapore) and onshore banking markets (such as Korea)—to obtain a clear understanding of how MNBs exploit their proprietary advantages and market opportunities, as specified in the model, in actual settings.

A summary and the conclusions are set forth in chapter 7, including managerial and policy implications of the findings of the study and recommendations for further research.

# 2

# Scope and Nature of Multinational Banking Operations

One of the most significant developments in the banking industry since the early 1970s has been the substantial expansion of multinational banking. The private banking sector has become an important part of the international monetary system and in many respects has shown itself to be more flexible and adaptable than official monetary arrangements in response to the substantial structural changes in the world economy and financial system since the 1970s. The role of multinational commercial banks in successfully recycling the petro-dollar surpluses to many deficit-ridden countries is a new feature in the multinational banking scene hardly expected from their traditional performance. Equally significant is their successful provision of the financial services necessitated by the substantial increase in international trade and foreign direct investment.

The pattern of multinational banking that has evolved since the early 1970s is distinctly different from the pattern prior to that time. First, the growth rate has been dramatic. Total assets of overseas branches of U.S. banks, which are the dominant group among multinational banks, and the operations of which are comprehensively and systematically documented, rose from US$35.3 billion in 1969 to US$476.5 billion in 1983. The number of U.S. banks with overseas branches jumped to 195 in 1983 from 53 in 1969. In 1960, assets of overseas branches of U.S. banks totaled US$3.5 billion and the number of U.S. banks operating abroad was only eight.

Second, the predominance of multinational corporations and official institutions in the international financial markets during the period brought about a change of emphasis from overseas retail banking to international wholesale banking. The role of the U.S. dollar in international payment and the growth of U.S. foreign direct investment enabled U.S. banks to become the dominant group amongst multinational banks. The increased importance of sovereign lending and the remarkable growth of Eurocurrency markets are a result of this change of emphasis.

Third, a new generation of multinational banks has emerged. Previously, a few large banks from the United States, the United Kingdom, Canada, and France had dominated the international banking markets. But since the 1970s, the international banking markets have been increasingly penetrated by a new generation of MNBs—medium-sized U.S. banks (both regional and money-center banks), Japanese banks, some second-tier Canadian and Continental European banks, and banks from Singapore, Hong Kong, and several less developed countries (LDCs). Growth and geographical diversification of international trade and foreign direct investment, increased integration of national financial markets, and various limitations on domestic expansion in the banks' home countries may be responsible for this phenomenon. The result is increased competition and narrowed interest margins (or spread) during the periods of higher interest rates and declining loan demand since the late 1970s.

The fourth difference is the increased interpenetration of developed countries' MNBs into each other's territory since the seventies, with the exception of offshore markets in developing countries. But the direction is now beginning to move slightly back toward LDCs again. Before the 1970s, the general direction of MNB moves had been from developed countries to developing countries where few established indigenous banks had existed and a significant share of foreign direct investments from developed regions had been located.

The increased importance and the new role of MNBs in the international financial markets have created some problems for MNBs themselves and for the international financial system. Stiffer competition in the more competitive markets has posed problems of lower profitability of foreign operations.[1] Increased involvement in sovereign lending has increased the vulnerability of MNBs as some LDCs face difficulties in repaying their debts from MNBs. Heavy lending of MNBs to several LDCs has widened the potential scope of problems that might occur in both domestic and multinational banking markets by defaults of any of these countries (table 2-1). Occasional rescheduling and refinancing arrangements between MNBs and debtor countries show the efforts of both sides to avoid the worst outcomes of this vulnerable relationship.

In this chapter, the nature and scope of multinational banking—types of multinational involvement, characteristics of major multinational banking activities, and current issues facing multinational banking—will be examined.

## Characteristics of a Multinational Bank

*Types of Multinational Banking Involvement*

The involvement of a bank in international financial markets can take place in a number of ways. Major types of international involvement currently found

Table 2-1.  Exposure of Nine Largest U.S. Commercial Banks to
Non-OPEC Developing Countries

| | December 1977 | | June 1982 | |
|---|---|---|---|---|
| | In billions of dollars | As a % of capital | In billions of dollars | As a % of capital |
| Brazil | 7.4 | 40% | 12.3 | 52% |
| Mexico | 5.9 | 32% | 13.6 | 57% |
| Korea | 2.2 | 12% | 5.1 | 21% |
| Argentina | 1.7 | 9% | 5.6 | 24% |
| Philippines | 1.3 | 7% | 3.7 | 16% |
| Taiwan | 1.8 | 10% | 2.7 | 11% |
| Sub-total (Six major borrowers) | 20.3 | 110% | 43.0 | 181% |
| Total (all non-OPEC developing countries) | 28.7 | 156% | 60.3 | 222% |

Source:  Board of Governors of the Federal Reserve System, quoted in Porzecanski (1981), p. 15.
Morgan Guaranty Trust Co., *World Financial Markets,* February 1983.
*Federal Reserve Bulletin,* September 1983.

among banks are correspondent relationships, representative offices, agencies, branches, subsidiaries, and consortium banks. Other than these major types, international banking involvement can often be realized through the establishment of the international department at the home office or specialized corporations, such as the Edge Act corporation of U.S. banks. However, international involvement via the international department cannot be said to be multinational banking as defined earlier, since such involvement does not accompany the cross-border transfer of financial, technological, and managerial resources. It is often the case that the choice of the type of foreign operation open to a bank is limited by the regulatory requirements of both host and home countries. But other factors relating to a bank's global strategy also decisively influence this choice. Furthermore, as in the case of the selection of the organizational structure of a firm in general, "no single route is the best for all countries and all conditions."[2] For example, the Chase Manhattan Bank has utilized a variety of methods and approaches, including the purchase of existing banks with trained manpower in Southeast Asia, joint ventures in Latin America, new branches in the Caribbean area, and a worldwide network of correspondents.

A bank's choice among these alternatives depends on relative advantages in terms of external factors, such as regulatory requirements of both host and home countries, general market conditions in host countries, as well as bank-specific internal factors. The bank-specific internal factors generally considered in selecting the appropriate organizational form include: (1) amount of investment required, (2) return on investment, (3) type and volume of foreign business, (4) control over operations, (5) referral business, (6) taxation, (7) new business, (8) flexibility of operation, (9) controls by host country, and (10) manpower requirements.[3] Table 2-2 shows the relative advantages of the various organizational forms of U.S. banks in terms of these ten factors, and major organizational forms will be explained in more detail below.

*Correspondent relationship.* The correspondent relationship frequently is used by banks that are involved in international banking but, given their size, cannot afford the set-up costs of an operation in foreign markets, or that feel the size of their dealings with a particular foreign market does not warrant establishing an office there for the delivery of a specific service. This is the simplest type of international banking involvement and can be formed simply by "an exchange of letters specifying activities to be carried out, conditions to be followed, and fees to be paid."[4] A correspondent relationship acts as a kind of sales agency for the bank that wants to engage in international banking activities. It is generally used to facilitate and perform transactions with overseas customers (acceptance of drafts, settlement of letters of credit, etc.), to clear balances with other banking institutions, and to exchange credit information about particular markets.

This type of involvement does not require a cross-border transfer of capital, managerial, and technological resources from home countries and, thus, no physical banking presence is required. Any transactions between correspondents are performed on an arm's length basis, as predetermined in correspondent contracts. The main objects of transactions between correspondents are usually the execution of certain banking services and the provision of information on particular customers (or prospective customers) and markets. The delivery of such services is exchanged with the payment of service fees. Ordinarily a service fee is deducted from a service-requesting bank's funds on deposit with the foreign correspondent bank. In this sense, it is equivalent to international trading activities of manufacturing firms, as international banking operations are conducted from the head office. In a correspondent relationship, the traded goods are the execution of certain banking services or the provision of information, whereas it is usually merchandise in the form of tangible goods in the case of manufacturing firms.

The correspondent approach has the advantages of not requiring any substantial investment in international banking facilities and manpower. However, it is a relatively inflexible form and offers only limited potential for developing new business. Correspondent banks tend to be interested primarily in their own benefits and are less likely to be very active on behalf of their counterparts. As banking services are basically contact-based, some kind of banking presence is necessary to provide such services adequately. Furthermore, recent developments in communications seem to make a correspondent relationship less necessary as some of the banking activities which used to be done via the correspondent route can be performed directly from bank head offices. The correspondent relationship is a useful mechanism in simple international banking, but not in multinational banking. Once a bank moves from simple international banking to multinational banking, it needs a banking presence in particular overseas markets in which it intends to have operations—representative office, agency, branch, subsidiary or consortium bank.

*Representative office.* The first move towards multinational banking usually materializes with the establishment of a representative office. Generally a representative office is not permitted by the host country government to conduct a full range of banking activities, the major prohibition being against the receipt of deposits and the direct extension of credits. The office is essentially for sales and service. Its major functions are referring new business prospects and opening up new sources of local information. Furthermore, it may be the only means of direct banking representation in a country that limits or prohibits branches of foreign banks or foreign ownership of banks.

Representative office operations usually keep their correspondent relationship with local banks intact. The office channels information and customers to the head office or to any offices within its banking network. It plays an important role in the bank's development of knowledge on the local market. Although it is the least expensive and most flexible way to enter foreign markets, its limited capacity to conduct major banking activities of deposit taking and lending tends to allow it only a transitional status to multinational banking proper. It usually precedes the establishment of more extensive forms such as an agency, a branch, or a subsidiary.

*Agency.* An agency is a banking office that transfers and lends funds but cannot take deposits from domestic sources in the host country and is an integral part of the parent bank. As it cannot accept domestic deposits, it usually is exempted from various official regulations with which a full-fledged bank must comply in the host country. For example, in the United States an agency of a foreign bank usually is not subject to legal fractional reserve requirements, Regulation Q, or close scrutiny by state authorities. It may make commercial and industrial loans, but is generally prohibited from making consumer loans. As it can provide only such limited banking services, its customers are mostly

Table 2-2. Analysis of Relative Advantages from Alternative Organizational Forms of U.S. Banks

| Advantage | Correspondent | International Department | Agency and Representative Office | Overseas Branch | Edge Act Corporation | Foreign Affiliate Majority Owned | Foreign Affiliate Minority Owned |
|---|---|---|---|---|---|---|---|
| 1. Amount of investment required | None | Moderate | Moderate | Substantial | Substantial | Moderate | Moderate |
| 2. Return on investment | DEPENDS ON OPERATIONS | | | | | | |
| 3. Type and volume of foreign business | Correspondent executes for U.S. bank | General international banking & servicing multinational clients | Source of information | General intl. banking and Euro-dollars | Out-of-state intl. dept. | Variety of financial services and joint ventures | Variety of financial services and joint ventures |
| 4. Control over operation | None | Direct control & leverage over Correspondent | Possiblity of influence over Correspondent | Direct control exists | Direct control exists | Substantial control | Minor control |
| 5. Referral business | On reciprocal basis | Minor | Positive by location | Most favourable | Most favourable | Potential depends on relation with parent | Minor |

Table 2-2 (continued)

| Advantage | Correspondent | International Department | Agency and Representative Office | Overseas Branch | Edge Act Corporation | Foreign Affiliate Majority Owned | Foreign Affiliate Minority Owned |
|---|---|---|---|---|---|---|---|
| 6. Taxation | Not applicable | Income is part of head office earnings | | Must pay foreign tax | | Tax is payable on fifteen percent of dividend paid by subsidiary | |
| 7. New business | From correspondent on reciprocal basis | Favourable | Favourable | Most favourable | Most favourable | Some potential exists | Limited potential |
| 8. Flexibility of operation | Relatively inflexible | Small amount of flexibility | Relatively inflexible | High degree of flexibility | Most flexible | Some flexibility | Inflexible |
| 9. Controls by host country | Not applicable | Not applicable | May be only means of direct representation in foreign country | May prohibit branch | May limit some activities | May limit foreign ownership | May limit foreign ownership |
| 10. Manpower | No requirement | Requirement depends on size | Some manpower required | May involve heavy commitment | Substantial commitment | Minor | Minor |

*A minimum 10 per cent ownership is required for applicability of the foreign tax credit.

Source: Francis A. Lees, International Banking and Finance (New York: Halsted Press, 1974), pp. 70-72.

By permission of MacMillan, London and Basingstock.

banks and businesses, particularly affiliate firms of the home country companies, rather than individuals. It usually emphasizes financing of foreign trade, such as handling letters of credit and bills of exchange, between the home and host countries as it does not have extensive customer base and domestic deposit sources in the host country.

Without any domestic deposit sources in the host country, an agency usually relies on funds transferred from its head and related offices and funds borrowed in the host interbank markets. Reliance on the latter source seems to be more prominent in the developed host markets than in the less developed host markets. In the United States, agencies of foreign banks increasingly rely on the U.S. interbank markets for their funding sources.[5] This raises some questions about the validity of the rationale behind prohibiting deposit acceptance by the agency if a major rationale behind the restriction is the protection of domestic depositors.

To some banks, this type of involvement may be more desirable than a branch in terms of effectiveness. To banks whose foreign branches do not or cannot engage in substantial domestic deposit-accepting activities for one reason or another—even though they are legally allowed to do so—an agency which is relatively less regulated and easier to establish may be a good alternative. Currently, the agency is one of the most common forms of multinational involvement of foreign banks in the United States (table 2-3).

*Branch.* The major difference between an agency and a branch is that a branch can accept domestic deposits while an agency cannot. A branch can offer a full range of banking services, is an integral part of the parent bank, has the full backing of the parent, and its creditors have claims on assets of the bank as a whole. It is subject to all the legal limitations which exist for the parent bank.

Aside from the advantages of being able to solicit domestic deposits, a branch enables the parent bank to maintain maximum control over its operations in the host country. A branch usually has less stringent limits on its lending capacity than a subsidiary since the limits are calculated on the basis of the capital of the parent bank. Furthermore, a branch has an advantage of name identification with the parent bank, whereas a correspondent relationship and a subsidiary form do not have such an advantage.

But a branch is usually subject to much more stringent regulatory examination than an agency. The branch necessitates a higher set-up cost and a higher commitment of manpower than other forms of banking. Moreover, the permission to accept domestic deposits might not result in the kind of advantage a bank expects. Various economic and noneconomic factors might prevent a bank from exploiting such an advantage fully. With limited branch networks and the disadvantage of less familiarity with the host markets, a branch of a foreign bank might not have enough deposit base to justify the

Table 2-3.  Growth Patterns in the Types of Foreign Bank Operation, 1972-83 (Number of offices)

| | November 1972 | November 1973 | November 1974 | November 1975 | November 1976 | November 1977 | April 1978 | December 1981 | December 1982 | December 1983 |
|---|---|---|---|---|---|---|---|---|---|---|
| Agencies | 50 | 62 | 70 | 81 | 91 | 110 | 123 | 195 | 188 | 177 |
| Branches | 26 | 32 | 50 | 64 | 70 | 98 | 106 | 194 | 221 | 260 |
| Subsidiaries | 25 | 27 | 29 | 33 | 34 | 35 | 39 | 52 | N.A. | N.A. |
| Investment Companies | 3 | 3 | 3 | 4 | 5 | 5 | 5 | N.A. | N.A. | N.A. |
| Total | 104 | 124 | 152 | 182 | 200 | 248 | 273 | 441 | 409 | 437 |

Source:  Board of Governors of the Federal Reserve System, released June 1978.
Federal Reserve Bank of New York, *Quarterly Review* (Summer 1982), p. 50.
*Federal Reserve Bulletin*, various issues.

Table 2-4.    Main Forms of Foreign Presence of 30 Largest
U.S. Banks, 1974

|  | Number | Percent | Amount (in millions of dollars) | Percent |
|---|---|---|---|---|
| Branches | 616 | 66.5 | 132,546 | 85.1 |
| Bank subsidiaries | 122 | 13.2 | 19,910 | 12.8 |
| Finance company subsidiaries | 156 | 16.8 | 2,650 | 1.7 |
| Other subsidiaries | 33 | 3.6 | 678 | 0.4 |
| Total | 927 | 100.0 | 155,784 | 100.0 |

Source:    *Financial Institutions and the Nation's Economy.* Book II, Committee on Banking, Currency and Housing, House of Representatives, 94th Congress, Second Session 1976.

operation economically. Oftentimes, lack of a sufficient domestic deposit base would pinch a branch's profitability when the lending market becomes lean. The legal status of a branch poses another potential disadvantage compared to a subsidiary. As a branch does not have its own independent legal personality, the parent bank is responsible for any actions by the branch under the host law, which is not the case for a subsidiary.

Despite these disadvantages, the branch and the agency have been the most preferred forms of presence in foreign markets due to their flexibility and operational scope. This preference is noticeable both among U.S. banks operating abroad and non-U.S. MNBs with a presence in the U.S. market (tables 2-4 and 2-5).

*Subsidiary.* A subsidiary is a banking office which is incorporated in the host country and usually can conduct all the banking activities allowed to domestic banks of the host country, with some exceptions.[6] Unlike an agency or a branch, it is a separate legal entity from the parent bank. The subsidiary form of involvement is often used when the host country does not permit any branch or agency establishment; some host countries allow foreign banks to operate only through the subsidiary form.[7]

A bank usually has some degree of control over its subsidiaries in a host country, the degree depending upon the level of ownership, which varies from a minority interest to 100 percent ownership. A subsidiary usually requires a higher capitalization than a branch for a given size of operations, as its loan limit is a function of its own capital. Acquisition of a minority interest in a foreign banking affiliate may, however, require only a modest equity investment. A minority interest offers little opportunity for control and limited

Table 2-5. Main Forms of Presence of Foreign Banks in the U.S. Market

| | November 1972 | | | | March 1980 | | | |
|---|---|---|---|---|---|---|---|---|
| | Number | Percent of Total | Total Assets (millions of Dollars) | Percent of Total | Number | Percent of Total | Total Assets (millions of Dollars) | Percent of Total |
| Agencies | 50 | 50 | 13,635 | 59.3 | 165 | 50.1 | 62,227 | 35.6 |
| Branches | 26 | 26 | 5,302 | 23.0 | 127 | 38.6 | 85,889 | 49.4 |
| Subsidiaries | 25 | 25 | 4,064 | 17.7 | 37 | 11.3 | 25,778 | 15.0 |
| | 101 | 101 | 23,001 | 100.0 | 329 | 100.0 | 173,894 | 100.0 |

| | December 1983 | | | |
|---|---|---|---|---|
| | Number | Percent of Total | Total Assets (millions of Dollars) | Percent of Total |
| Agencies | 177 | 40.5 | 52,354 | 22.9 |
| Branches | 260 | 59.5 | 176,063 | 77.1 |
| Subsidiaries | N.A. | N.A. | N.A. | N.A. |
| | 437 | 100.0 | 228,417 | 100.0 |

Source: L.G. Goldberg and A. Saunders (1981), p. 367.
Federal Reserve Bulletin, various issues.

potential for developing new business through referrals, but it does provide the parent bank with the prospects for developing closer business and banking connections in the host country more easily than might be possible by going it alone or establishing a new banking institution.

*Nature of Multinational Banking Activities*

Most multinational banking activities of MNBs are basically an extension of banking activities performed by banks on the domestic level.[8] The fact that international financial intermediation involves intercountry and intercurrency flows (and hence problems and issues peculiar to this process) does not obscure the fundamental principles of financial intermediation that are common to both the domestic and international dimension. The apparent "uniqueness" of multinational banking activities comes from their intercountry and intercurrency intermediation process. Differences in monetary standards, regulatory frameworks, business practices, and sociocultural environments among the various countries in which MNBs operate seem to create this uniqueness. The concept and reality of political risk—the risks of war, revolution, expropriation, and unavailability of foreign exchange—and currency risk complicate multinational banking activities and make them look unique compared with uninational domestic banking activities.

The nature and scope of multinational banking activities are different depending on the types of international involvement of MNBs. The nature and scope of activities of a foreign banking subsidiary may be different from those of a foreign branch or agency. A foreign banking subsidiary can conduct any banking activities allowed under the host country regulations in the host market regardless of the home country regulations governing the parent bank. A foreign branch usually is not allowed to conduct any banking activities which are prohibited under the home country regulations, even though these activities are allowed under the host country regulations. A good example is that a foreign branch of U.S. commercial banks cannot perform investment banking activities in a foreign market even though these activities are allowed under the host country regulations. But a banking subsidiary of a U.S. commercial bank in the host country, in this case, can conduct the investment banking activities. The nature and scope also vary across individual MNBs and host markets. Therefore, in this section, multinational banking activities will be explained, centering mainly on those of foreign branches of MNBs, as a branch form of involvement is the most typical and preferred form of banking presence in foreign markets. Furthermore, activities of foreign banking subsidiaries are so diverse among them that it is almost meaningless to try to find any commonality from them. They range from traditional banking activities to manufacturing and tourism activities.

Like banking activities on the domestic level, multinational banking activities largely consist of credit extension, deposit acceptance, and other related banking services. Credit extension is the principal service offered by foreign branches of MNBs. Deposit acceptance tends to be relatively less emphasized at foreign branches of MNBs for various reasons, with some exceptions in offshore markets.

*Multinational credit extension activities.* Credit extension activities not only provide the major source of a bank's revenue, but also represent its image in the sense that credit and loan quality are regarded as the barometer of banking success. They include direct loans, acceptances for the account of foreign banks, claims on foreign banks and nonbanks in the process of collections, and other types of outstanding claim on foreigners resulting from transactions, loans, or clearing activities. Multinational credit extension can be done by either the head offices of MNBs or their foreign branches. It can be conducted in either local or foreign currencies, but mostly in U.S. dollars and a number of "hard" currencies of the major industrial countries. It can be a truly international one, that is cross-border lending, or local lending in the country where a foreign branch of an MNB operates. However, in fundamental aspects, it is not much different from uninational domestic credit extension. Only its "multinationality" adds some characteristics to it.

Borrowers from MNBs are typically multinational corporations (usually from industrial countries), banks, and foreign governments or government agencies (usually of less developed countries). Recently, big corporations from less developed countries have also emerged as an important borrower group. Relative share of each borrower group of major U.S. MNBs is shown in table 2-6. Loans to these groups of borrowers have several characteristics distinct from domestic loans largely due to the nature of these customer groups. Though the purposes of these borrowers may cover a broad range, they commonly are to finance large industrial projects, general economic development plans, or balance of payments deficits. This naturally requires loans to be big and of medium-term nature. Lendings of MNBs are actually of large size and of a term nature, with average size occasionally running up to over US $1 billion and final maturities stretching as far as ten years. Due to the size and maturities of MNB loans, interest rates are normally determined on a floating basis. Interest rates usually float at a fixed spread over the costs of funding the loan through the purchase of deposits in the market. The floating rate system is a shrewd response on the part of MNBs to reduce interest rate risks. In a market with volatile interest rates, fixed-rate term loans can increase the vulnerability of MNBs to any changes in interest rates. The spread over the cost of funds is presumably sufficient to cover expenses, a loan loss reserve, and contribution to profits. The spread is generally a function of perceived credit risk and

Table 2-6.  Types of International Loans and Deposits of Major U.S. MNBs
(As of end of 1983, in million U.S. dollars)

| | Bank of America | Chase Manhattan | Citicorp | First Chicago | Manufacturers Hanover | J.P. Morgan |
|---|---|---|---|---|---|---|
| **LOANS** | | | | | | |
| 1. Loans to Banks & Financial Institutions | 3,855 (14%) | 4,656 (13%) | 5,914 (15%) | 1,873 (24%) | 6,988 (33%) | 3,525 (15%) |
| 2. Loans to Governments & Official Institutions | 3,333 (12%) | 2,735 (8%) | 4,074 (10%) | 1,979 (25%) | 3,810 (18%) | 2,755 (12%) |
| 3. Commercial & Industrial Loans | 18,412 (67%) | 24,516 (70%) | 27,592 (70%) | 3,741 (48%) | 10,335 (49%) | 12,660 (55%) |
| 4. All Other Loans | 2,074 (7%) | 3,165 (9%) | 1,822 (5%) | 258 (3%) | – | 4,184 (18%) |
| Total Loans | 27,674 (100%) | 35,072 (100%) | 39,402 (100%) | 7,851 (100%) | 21,133 (100%) | 23,124 (100%) |
| **DEPOSITS** | | | | | | |
| 1. Foreign Governments & Official Institutions | 2,281 (6%) | 3,153 (9%) | – | 1,377 (10%) | 3,533 (21%) | 2,928 (16%) |
| 2. Banks in Foreign Countries | 13,767 (38%) | 10,286 (28%) | 19,353 (39%) | 4,380 (32%) | 8,566 (51%) | 7,246 (38%) |
| 3. Other Foreign Demand Deposits | 1,620 (4%) | 2,792 (8%) | 6,667 (13%) | 240 (2%) | 325 (2%) | 1,029 (5%) |
| 4. Other Foreign Savings & Time Deposits | 18,610 (51%) | 20,032 (55%) | 24,008 (48%) | 7,633 (56%) | 4,404 (26%) | 7,678 (41%) |
| Total Deposits | 36,278 (100%) | 36,263 (100%) | 50,028 (100%) | 13,630 (100%) | 16,828 (100%) | 18,881 (100%) |

Source:  Individual banks' annual reports and 10-K reports.

competitive factors. But during most of the period since the middle 1970s with the exception of a period from mid-1974 to late 1975, competition dominated and often overturned these theoretical pricing considerations.

Multinational credit extension entails unique political and currency risks which do not exist in domestic lending. Political risk usually refers to all matters political, ranging from minor but unforeseen regulations that might be imposed on the bank or the borrower to the expropriation of property and expulsion from the country. Currency risk is concerned with convertibility and the stability of the monetary unit denominating the loans. However, as multinational loans are denominated mostly in U.S. dollars and several "hard" currencies, risk of inconvertibility is relatively minor. Foreign exchange rate risks are the major currency risks. This fact renders foreign exchange management operations one of the major functions of MNBs. However, any impacts on expected earnings of MNB customers resulting from currency fluctuations do not constitute currency risks. They belong to credit risks which both domestic and multinational banks face commonly when lending. Credit extension to foreign governments or government agencies poses special risks to MNBs. Loans to governments are generally unsecured and MNBs have relatively little recourse for recovering them in case of default.

The major part of multinational direct lending takes the form of syndication among many banks, often as many as ten or more. Syndication achieves many purposes: "it limits the exposure of individual banks, makes available loan participations to banks which do not have the marketing apparatus necessary to generate the business themselves, and brings new lenders into a relationship with the borrower."[9] It also makes it easier to raise funds for large-scale loans. Recently, it has become an important source of fee-income for the bank or banks which originate and manage the loan. Usually the large U.S. money-center banks, major British banks, and, recently, the larger West German, Canadian, and Japanese banks dominate the multinational syndicated loan markets. An interesting development observable in the markets recently is that some popular borrowers increasingly become in effect their own investment bankers and dictate not only loan terms but the actual participants in the loan,[10] which was a rare occurrence until recently.

Another important aspect related to international credit extension operations of MNBs is their participation in the interbank markets in major international financial centers. This is related to their funding operations as well. The placing of money in time deposits with other banks, commonly called interbank placements, represents a substantial part of the business of MNB branches located in major international financial centers. This high volume, low margin business provides a convenient opportunity for banks with no readily available borrowers to dispose efficiently of temporarily idle funds, or for those banks with no extensive deposit base to secure funds for their loan demands. The interbank markets serve the crucial role of ensuring the allocational efficiency and flexibility of the international money market.[11] But sometimes a substantial proportion of interbank deposit trading appears to take place simply for the sake of the banks' continuing to appear as active participants in the market, not necessarily for the purpose of matching ultimate borrowers' and lenders' needs.[12] Actually, virtually all banks dependent on offshore financial markets for funding their multinational loan portfolio engage in both ends of the interbank market.

Another significant part of credit extension activities of MNBs is local lending in their branches' indigenous markets. It is mostly done in local currencies and is usually of wholesale nature. It used to be, and is still in many less developed host markets, one of the most lucrative businesses of MNB foreign branches. In the markets where domestic interest rates are significantly higher than rates in international financial markets, and which experience chronic excess demands for credits, local lending by MNB branches which have an easy access to cheaper funds in international financial markets or within their banking networks surely is an attractive business. But the opportunities seem not to be what they once were, and they continue to diminish, as banking industries in less developed countries are becoming increasingly competitive and technically advanced, and it is becoming less difficult for them to gain access to international credit markets.

The degree to which MNB branches engage in local lending varies greatly from country to country. Some countries restrict the extent to which foreign branches can engage in this activity, in terms of size and type of loan. Others simply have few eligible borrowers. In industrial countries, well-entrenched local banks do not leave many opportunities for local lending business to foreign bank branches.

Financing international trade is also one of the important aspects of credit extension activities of MNB branches in some countries. Trade financing is done largely by MNB branches in onshore banking markets, though MNB branches in offshore banking markets engage in this business indirectly. Offshore MNB branches are involved in trade financing indirectly in the sense that they place hard currencies with banks from less developed countries which in turn use the funds for financing trade. The trade financing activities of MNB branches in onshore markets are mostly import financing. They extend hard currency credits to local importers to settle their import transactions through the issuance of letters of credit.

Other than those activities discussed, MNBs engage in such credit extension related activities as the creation of bankers' acceptances, the provision of guarantees, loan commitments and lines of credit, and the collection of drafts. Though the size of these related activities is not substantial compared to the principal multinational credit extension activities, they remain important elements of multinational banking activities.

*Multinational Funding Activities.* Funding activities provide the basic raw material of any banking operation. They help a bank to generate earning assets. A bank usually has various funding sources which differ in their costs and duration. A portfolio of quality funding sources is as important as a quality loan portfolio to the success of a bank on both the domestic and the multinational level. Major primary funding sources in domestic banking usually include customer deposits, shareholders' investment, and profits. They also have secondary sources such as public borrowings in financial markets, inter- and intrabank borrowings, and collection of outstanding loans. Often the secondary sources are found to be more important than the primary sources. In multinational banking, however, funding sources are not as widely diversified as they are in domestic banking. Head office's investment, Eurocurrency deposits, local deposits, interbank borrowings, and intrabank borrowings usually constitute the major funding sources of MNB foreign branches. The relative importance of individual sources varies among MNBs and the locations of their foreign branches. Table 2-7 shows the relative importance of major funding sources of foreign branches of U.S. MNBs. Interbank borrowings have been the most important funding source of the foreign branches of U.S. MNBs, but the importance of customer deposits, both of local and foreign currencies, and intrabank borrowings has increased continuously.

Most interbank borrowings are raised by foreign branches located in major international money markets. Interbank borrowings are possible from the head offices with the help of modern telecommunication facilities, without necessarily locating banking offices in major international money markets. However, to have an active, physical presence in the market in close proximity to the lending banks obviously has its advantages. Moreover, presence in major international money markets offers advantages in accepting deposits in those markets. Especially for U.S. banks, overseas branches enable them to quote competitive interest rates for deposits in those markets as they can escape the Federal Reserve Board's reserve requirements and interest rate limitations. These are applicable to deposits accepted by banks in the U.S., but not at their overseas branches. Although interbank funds are an important and efficient funding source, they can be highly volatile and uncertain, as the events of 1974 demonstrated. They can be withdrawn at any time with short notice and are quite vulnerable to slight changes in interest rates. Furthermore, the size of interbank borrowings as a funding source should be interpreted carefully as most MNBs participate in both interbank lendings and interbank borrowings, often with the same banks.

Customer deposits are also an important funding source. They are one of the cheapest sources of money among all funding sources. It is generally recognized that the more a bank's assets are funded with customer deposits, the greater the profit margin the bank will enjoy. Customer deposits are also a

Table 2-7. Share of Major Funding Sources of Foreign Branches of U.S. MNBs
(In millions of U.S. dollars at year end)

| | 1973 | 1974 | 1976 | 1978 | 1979 | 1980 | 1981 | 1982 | 1983 |
|---|---|---|---|---|---|---|---|---|---|
| Liabilities to nonbanks[1] | 31,981 (26.2%) | 46,547 (30.6%) | 64,652 (29.5%) | 90,894 (29.6%) | 111,082 (30.5%) | 124,666 (31.1%) | 130,557 (28.2%) | 134,177 (28.6%) | 146,730 (30.8%) |
| Liabilities to the parent bank & other branches of parent bank | 19,855 (16.3%) | 32,750 (21.6%) | 64,143 (29.2%) | 96,150 (31.3%) | 102,131 (28.0%) | 114,951 (28.7%) | 142,740 (30.8%) | 165,812 (35.3%) | 169,592 (35.6%) |
| Liabilities to other banks | 65,389 (53.7%) | 65,676 (43.2%) | 83,880 (38.2%) | 109,880 (35.8%) | 136,817 (37.6%) | 146,220 (36.5%) | 144,103 (31.2%) | 130,265 (27.7%) | 121,999 (25.6%) |
| Other | 4,641 (3.8%) | 6,933 (4.6%) | 6,747 (3.1%) | 9,871 (3.3%) | 14,203 (3.9%) | 14,673 (3.7%) | 45,447 (9.8%) | 39,458 (8.4%) | 38,218 (8.0%) |
| Total | 121,866 | 151,906 | 219,422 | 306,795 | 364,233 | 400,510 | 462,847 | 469,712 | 476,539 |

1. Liabilities to "other banks in the U.S." are included. The source classified liabilities of foreign branches of U.S. banks to the United States into "liabilities to parent banks" and "liabilities to other" until 1977.

Source:    Federal Reserve Bulletin, various issues.

relatively stable funding source. They can be foreign currency deposits (Eurocurrency deposits) or local currency deposits. Major Eurocurrency depositors at MNBs are typically multinational corporations, foreign governments or government agencies, foreign central banks and foreign financial institutions. Relative share of each deposit group of U.S. MNBs is shown in table 2-6. A banking presence in the markets seems to create more substantial advantages in gathering Eurocurrency deposits than in the case of interbank borrowings at major international money markets. Deposit-taking operations generally require more personal and closer services than lending operations.

Local currency deposits usually do not constitute a significant funding source in multinational banking. Local deposit gathering is particularly difficult for branches of foreign banks for several reasons. With a limited branch network, due to either lack of sufficient local businesses to warrant an extensive branch network or host government restrictions on branching, branches simply cannot cultivate a significant local deposit base. Moreover, some host governments do not permit them to accept local deposits at all, or prohibit certain kinds of local deposit. Local deposits are generally the most safe and economical funding source for local lending. With a lack of this source, most foreign branches of MNBs rely on other sources for local lending, often local currencies acquired from host central banks or commercial banks through swap arrangements for foreign currencies.

Intrabank borrowings provide another important funding source. Those foreign branches which are not located in major international financial centers rely heavily on borrowings from the head office and other sister branches for their operations. MNBs with an extensive and active network in major international financial centers are better able to meet this funding need of their foreign branches. Other than as an important funding source, intrabank borrowings are often employed for the purpose of transfer price manipulation.

As mentioned previously, the relative importance of these individual funding sources varies depending upon the nature of operations individual MNBs perform and the locations of their international operations. Each branch or MNB tries to develop its own optimal portfolio of funding sources. This process is becoming an increasingly important function in multinational banking. Generally, MNBs with extensive networks worldwide and better accessibility to a variety of funding sources seem to have better maneuverability in their portfolio selection.

*Other related activities.* Other than credit extension and funding activities, MNBs engage in various fee-earning related activities in overseas markets. These fee-earning activities are becoming increasingly important sources of bank revenue, as income derived independently of a capital base is one of the few means by which an MNB beset by rapidly rising costs of operation, limited lending spreads, and a presumed leverage ceiling can produce a reasonably attractive return on stockholder funds.

Typical of the fee-earning activities of MNBs are various traditional international banking activities, such as letters of credit, foreign drafts and collections, international money transfers, and operation of correspondent banking clearing accounts. Together with some of the traditional domestic fee-earning banking activities such as domestic money transfers and credit investigations, these activities represent a significant fee-earning business for most MNB foreign branches. Though these relatively labor-intensive activities have been avoided by most Eurobanks in major international money centers, which consider themselves wholesale banks with a limited client base, the experience of several banks indicates that these more traditional activities can produce a useful profit.[13]

Foreign exchange business is a second major peripheral multinational banking activity. Large MNBs usually conduct four basic types of foreign exchange business:[14] (1) retail-oriented foreign currency drafts; (2) larger corporate transactions to fund subsidiaries in local currencies, to hedge or convert dividends from these subsidiaries, and to hedge fixed assets and liabilities; (3) correspondent bank business; and (4) interbank market making. Foreign exchange business is generally done in interbank markets. The first three types are basically fee-based activities for their customers. The last one is done basically to hedge a bank's foreign exchange exposure and to maintain its positions. The basic objective of foreign exchange operations is to provide a bank's customers with necessary foreign exchange and to hedge the bank's own foreign exchange risk exposure, though in the course of this operation a bank may gain or lose. Some banks, however, engage in interbank trading for a profit in addition to meeting the foreign exchange needs of their customers. Some banks have been quite successful in achieving this profit objective, while others have experienced substantial losses. However, as this involves risks, especially in periods of volatile foreign exchange rate movement, a bank needs to be cautious in performing foreign exchange operations for profit purposes. There have been some instances when foreign exchange operation losses caused irreparable damage to the safety of banks.[15] In major international money centers, foreign exchange trading is often combined with money market activity as banks borrow one currency and invest it in another on a short-term basis.

A third general area of fee-earning activity is the management or comanagement of syndicated Eurocurrency loans. This is an area where an MNB can combine its balance sheet strength, financial packaging skills, and marketing talents to earn management or front end fees. The size and frequency of these fees usually have been a function of market competitiveness and the attractions of the particular piece of business. During the borrower's markets of 1973 and 1978/79, prime borrowers such as big MNCs and well-regarded foreign central banks themselves brought together a willing group of MNB lenders under their own terms to which few participating banks could counterpropose. In contrast, during the lender's market of early 1975, management fees for less popular country credits rose to 1 percent flat and more.[16]

In the past, manager positions in syndicated Eurocurrency loans were usually limited to large MNBs, mostly large U.S. banks and their affiliates in major international money centers. Worldwide networks allowed these MNBs to generate and monitor business, and substantial balance sheet strength enabled them to take substantial portions of the loans. However, with the continued narrowing of spreads and the emergence of an aggressive group of new MNBs, these positions are being shared with MNBs from Japan, Europe, and Canada. The benefits of originating a successful syndication of a Eurocurrency loan are that (1) the originating bank generally retains a portion of the management fee or override for itself, and (2) the bank appears as lead or agent bank in the publicity tombstone. Currently the override for a lead manager usually amounts to about 0.125 percent of the total management fee (which typically is 1 percent of loan amount). Many large MNBs have separate merchant bank subsidiaries located in major international money centers to handle such loan syndication management, although some conduct this activity in their foreign branches or at the head office.

A final area of major fee-earning activities is international money management services for mostly multinational corporations. The service has its origins in domestic cash management. On the international level, it includes facilitating the cross-border flow and concentration of cash, advising and assisting in finding overseas investment opportunities for short-term surplus funds, and providing market information on particular foreign markets for corporate customers. A number of large MNBs have teams of experts to perform such services and are beginning to show increasing interest in them. Some of this kind of service is often provided without direct compensation. However, such activity serves a bank in a number of ways; generating income without burdening its balance sheet, providing a competitive edge in attracting customers, and enhancing the bank's overall relationship with its corporate customers.

Other than these activities, a number of noncommercial banking activities are being increasingly located in foreign branches of larger MNBs. Activities such as investment management, arrangement of back-to-back loans, project financing, leasing, new issues, mergers and acquisitions, and advice on fund raising and corporate restructuring are often performed at foreign branches of larger MNBs in major international money centers.

*Problems facing multinational banks.* Despite their impressive growth during the past decade, MNBs face several problems which, if not solved, might pose serious threats to their continued operation. Some problems have already begun to take their toll, while others are just emerging as serious threats to the continued success of MNBs. Some originate in developments external to the banks, like developments in the world economy, the international monetary system, and host government policies on MNBs. Others arise from internal sources. MNBs' operational patterns, competition in the market, and their financial structures are responsible for part of the problems. Increasingly, MNBs are beginning to take a hard look at their current multinational banking operations, and some have even begun to take "corrective" actions against some problems. This might not have been considered as seriously among MNBs about a decade ago, at least among larger MNBs.[17]

One of the primary problems is a deteriorating profitability of multinational banking operations. Table 2-8 shows the profitability of multinational banking operations of the ten most internationally active American banks. The average profit margin on international assets dropped from 0.52 percent in 1976 to 0.44 percent in 1979, rising again to 0.51 percent in 1983, while the average profit margin on domestic assets increased from 0.40 percent to 0.57 percent and 0.59 percent in the same period of time. Similar trends of declining profitability of multinational operations can also be found

Table 2-8.    Return on Domestic and International Assets at Ten Largest U.S. Commercial Banks

|  | 1976 Return on Assets | | 1979 Return on Assets | | 1983 Return on Assets | |
|---|---|---|---|---|---|---|
|  | Domestic | International | Domestic | International | Domestic | International |
| Citicorp | 0.4% | 0.8% | 0.5% | 0.5% | 0.8% | 0.7% |
| Bank of America | 0.1% | 0.4% | 0.7% | 0.6% | 0.3% | 0.6% |
| Chase Manhattan | 0.4% | 0.5% | 0.5% | 0.4% | 0.7% | 0.6% |
| Manufacturers Hanover | 0.3% | 0.6% | 0.4% | 0.5% | 0.5% | 1.0% |
| J.P. Morgan | 0.7% | 0.7% | 0.7% | 0.7% | 0.8% | 1.6% |
| Chemical | 0.3% | 0.4% | 0.4% | 0.3% | 0.6% | 0.7% |
| Bankers Trust | 0.2% | 0.4% | 0.3% | 0.4% | 0.9% | 0.5% |
| Continental Illinois | 0.6% | 0.2% | 0.7% | 0.3% | 0.4% | 0.1% |
| First Chicago | 0.7% | 0.4% | 0.7% | 0.03% | 0.7% | 0.2% |
| Security Pacific | 0.6% | 0.1% | 0.7% | 0.35% | 0.8% | 0.5% |
| Weighted Average | 0.40% | 0.52% | 0.57% | 0.44% | 0.59% | 0.51% |

Source:    Salomon Brothers, quoted in Porzecanski, A., "The International Financial Role of U.S. Commercial Banks: Past and Future," *Journal of Banking and Finance*, 5 (1981), p. 9.
Individual banks' annual reports and 10-K reports

among major European banks, though the evidence is not as graphic because most European banks can hide behind less demanding disclosure laws. However, Barclays Bank, Lloyds Bank International, and Union Bank of Switzerland admit either directly or indirectly a deteriorating profitability of their multinational banking operations.[18] In addition to the decline of the return on assets ratio (ROA) of multinational banking operations, the spreads between interest paid on foreign liabilities and interest earned on foreign assets is narrowing steadily (see figure 2-1). In 1975, for instance, Chase Manhattan Bank had a 2.02 percent spread between its overseas earning assets and interest-bearing liabilities, but this dropped to 1.66 percent in 1979 and 1.69 percent in 1982. Barclays went from 2.1 percent in 1978 to 1.3 percent and 1.2 percent in 1979 and 1980 respectively, and Citibank had a parallel decline.[19]

The deterioration is mostly ascribed to increased competition among MNBs and from indigenous banks and to world economic recession. Higher interest rates and a dearth of loan demand due to world economic recession are often cited as major causes for the loan spread squeeze. As banks usually face a faster increase in interest paid for funding than interest earned from lending during a period of rising interest rates, it is probable that higher interest rates may have squeezed the spreads. Scarcity of loan demand, with increasing competition among MNBs, may result in the narrower spreads in multinational lending. But profitability in domestic banking in major countries has increased, or at least not decreased, even though domestic banking markets face the same problems of high interest rates and economic recession. This suggests that higher interest rates and a dearth of loan demand are not sufficient explanations for lower profitability in multinational lending. This prompts one to seek further explanations of deteriorating profitability from increased competition among MNBs and indigenous banks in major markets. Profitability of major MNBs in the developed markets of Europe, North America, and Japan has experienced an especially severe deterioration recently.[20] The major reason behind this, according to most bankers, is the inability to cope with well-entrenched indigenous banks which in turn are themselves mostly MNBs. Spreads on lendings to large multinational corporations and governments are not much better. They have been driven lower and lower by excess liquidity, excess competition among MNBs and a sluggish world economy. Rates as low as 0.25 percent over LIBOR (London Interbank Offered Rates) have been reported for a recent ten-year standby credit, whereas a margin of at least 1.25 percent should be generated to make such a loan profitable considering costs and risks.[21] Similar trends are also prevalent in various fee-earning activities, such as trade-related banking, international correspondent banking, management of syndicated loans, and international cash management. Increased competition in multinational banking, particularly competition from Japanese and Arab banks, is largely

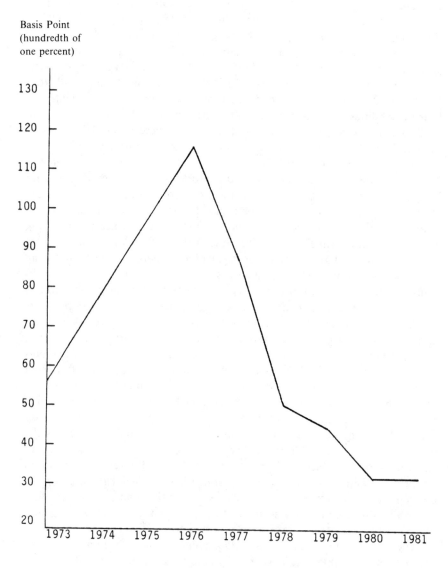

Figure 2-1. Lowest Spread for Individual Eurocurrency Loans[1]
(Fourth quarter of year)

Basis Point
(hundredth of
one percent)

1. Loans of US$50 million and over.
Source: OECD, *Financial Market Trends*, various issues.

responsible for the lower profitability, together with a sluggish world economy. Both groups of banks have advantages in competing with the U.S. and European banks. Japanese banks can offer low-priced loans since they can afford a lower ROA because of their thin capital structure. Arab banks have a preferential access to OPEC deposits and a substantial volume of assets to be redeposited.

Three major patterns are observable in the reaction of MNBs to deteriorating profitability. One reaction is to retreat or reassess multinational operations. For example, Bank of America has sold all but one of its offices in France and cut back some of its operations in Germany. First National Bank of Chicago has scaled down some parts of its European network. Several U.S. regional banks have withdrawn from their European operations. Some have pruned their relationships with those customers which do not provide sufficient return for services rendered. Another pattern of reaction is to divert emphasis toward higher risk and higher-spread business in the less developed nations of Latin America and the Far East, and to value-added services such as project lending. In this process, they tend to deemphasize their efforts in Western Europe and the U.S., where spreads are thin and markets are already overcrowded. They also tend to concentrate their resources on higher yielding but less creditworthy borrowers. Finally, some groups of banks continue to expand their multinational involvement, due sometimes to limitations on their domestic expansion. Several Dutch and French banks have sought overseas outlets mainly due to domestic credit ceilings and low profits. Other banks go abroad for less substantial reasons. Some Asian banks infected with multinational banking fever, to some extent, seek foreign expansion for much less substantial reasons.[22]

A second major problem, which flows from MNBs' response to the first, is the increased level of risk in multinational lending, particularly lending to LDC borrowers. MNBs by their nature are subject to different types of operating risk than purely domestic banks. The major operating risks of domestic banks are credit risk of their lending and interest spread risk. Credit risk arises from uncertainties about borrowers' abilities to honor the payments of interest and principal on schedule. Interest spread risk occurs whenever the interest rate rises, due to relative inflexibility of lending rate changes. But MNBs face additional risks other than credit and interest spread risks in their multinational operations. They face such risks as political risk and foreign exchange risk. Political risk occurs when an MNB becomes involved in a particular foreign country through ownership involvement, such as equity shares in local companies, bank branches, joint ventures, or other types of ownership interest. The risk is associated with the possibility that the continued ownership of the investment and the future flow of returns from it may be somehow impaired by political events of a particular country. Foreign exchange risk arises when economic or political events prevent the borrower from converting domestic currency into foreign currency to repay loans, and foreign exchange rate fluctuations create uncertainties in the real value of the loans repaid.

MNBs, due to the growth of their operations since the middle 1970s, are facing increased levels of country risk. Increased sovereign lending since the midseventies has exposed many MNBs to high sovereign credit risk for which most MNBs do not have any adequate evaluation system and reliable recourse in case of default. Already MNBs have experienced several rescheduling arrangements with Turkey, Zaire, Peru, Iran, Poland, Mexico and Argentina. This experience demonstrates the vulnerability of MNB lenders to a host of political and economic considerations which may oblige them, at a minimum, to wait an extended period until problems can be corrected. The experience has changed the attitude of MNBs toward sovereign lending and revealed a potential for a greater crisis. Until recently bankers argued that their claims would be the last to suffer in a rescheduling process considering the value attached to credibility in the international financial markets. In addition, even such a rescheduling would be less disastrous than the prospect of partial or total loss of principal lent to a failed private corporation or project.[23] However, after several rounds of rescheduling, this "countries-don't-go-bankrupt" assumption is no longer so comforting. Currently, the issue seems to be how much reserve should be established for problem loans to sovereign borrowers who are either unable to negotiate a mutually agreeable debt rescheduling or are incapable of servicing the newly rescheduled debt. Considering the possibilities of a "contagion" effect from several other highly indebted LDCs (table 2-9), adequate reserve accumulation, if not an outright write-off, would be a big burden for MNB profitability in the short run.

Moreover, the recent experience reveals a possibility of violent shifts or discontinuities in market psychology as a result of overreaction on the part of MNBs. MNB overreaction to a possible sovereign default might have a widespread ripple effect on sovereign borrowers who otherwise might be good debtors, which would be worse than one or two sovereign defaults. Presently, MNBs do not seem to have any reliable restraint mechanisms to avert such herd instinct within the system.

A third observable problem facing MNBs is the volatility of their funding sources. MNBs, especially foreign branches in major international money centers, rely heavily on short-term, high cost, volatile deposits and borrowings in interbank markets for their funding sources. The practice of converting such short-term and volatile funds into financial commitments of several years or more threatens the ability of MNBs to meet their obligations. Though they successfully surmounted the 1974 crisis of confidence with coordinated efforts of their central banks, there is no assurance that similar or more serious crises, accompanied by serious loan losses, will not recur in the future.

Table 2-9.    External Debts Owed to Banks by Selected Countries
(In billions of U.S. Dollars, year-end 1983)

|  | Total | % of 1982 GDP |
| --- | --- | --- |
| Mexico | 84.9 | 49.6% |
| Brazil | 73.7 | 29.6% |
| Argentina | 24.1 | 37.4% |
| Korea | 23.4 | 34.2% |
| Venezuela | 21.2 | 30.5% |
| Philippines | 14.6 | 36.8% |
| Yugoslavia | 14.5 | 21.3% |
| Indonesia | 13.2 | 14.7% |
| Egypt | 12.0 | 45.4% |
| Chile | 11.9 | 49.4% |

Source:    IMF, *International Capital Markets* (Occasional Paper #31, August 1984).
The World Bank, *World Development Report 1984.*

A fourth problem is host government restrictions on MNB activities in their countries. This poses a major problem for overseas branching operations, particularly at a time when more and more MNBs are trying to expand into the onshore banking markets of industrializing countries due to excess competition and lower profitability in developed and offshore banking markets. Some countries completely prohibit foreign banks from operating branches, while others allow branches but impose varying degrees of restrictions on their activities. The pattern of restrictions varies among countries and is difficult to attribute to any common characteristic such as level of economic development or geographic location. However, the basic rationale behind host restrictions on foreign banks seems to be to maintain "optimal" competition in their banking markets, though the nature of optimal competition is often quite vague.

The most common form of government control involves restraints on the domestic funding operations of foreign branches. Restrictions on acceptance of local deposits, access to central banks' rediscount facilities, participation in local interbank markets, and amounts of local currency convertible via swapping are typical host government restrictions on funding operations. This limits the ability of MNBs to participate in local currency lending, which is typically the most lucrative operation in onshore banking markets. Some countries even prohibit local currency lending, allowing only limited foreign currency lending and trade financing.

Other than such direct restrictions on funding operations, some governments control the number of branches an MNB can maintain within their countries. This restricts the MNB's funding operations indirectly, since without an extensive branch network, an MNB cannot attract sizable local deposits even though acceptance of local deposits is allowed.

The regulatory environment in home countries is also an important issue facing MNBs. Some regulations affect the multinational operations of home banks directly, some indirectly. For example, Swedish regulations allow Swedish banks to engage in banking activities in foreign markets only via a form of banking subsidiary. Some countries have regulations on the nature and kind of banking activities their banks can engage in, which usually regulate home banks' overseas activities as well. Regulations of a purely domestic nature may often affect home banks' overseas activities indirectly. Changes of regulations which result in changes in the competitive situation of domestic banking markets, for example, may significantly influence the multinational operations of the home banks which went overseas to overcome the limited opportunities for expansion in domestic markets. Relaxation of the current U.S. regulations on interstate banking would probably affect the multinational banking activities of U.S. banks significantly.

So far, the nature of major activities of MNBs and major challenges facing them have been explored. In the next section, the evolutionary patterns of MNB growth will be identified, using the experience of U.S. banks in multinational expansion. The experience of U.S. banks is the most important and comprehensive of any MNBs, so it provides a good case for studying the motivations and growth patterns of MNBs.

**Patterns of MNB Growth: The Case of U.S. Commercial Banks**

Until the period after the First World War most American banks, like American companies in general, traditionally had been quite ethnocentric, which produced a basic reluctance to "go international." Along with the sociocultural influences of the time, the rapidly growing domestic banking markets and relatively self-sufficient national economy did not generate much international push. In addition, U.S. banking regulations added deterrents to overseas banking. For example, national banks were prohibited from opening branches (domestic or foreign) until the passage of the Federal Reserve Act of 1913. But such traditional international banking activities as foreign exchange trading and the issuance of letters of credit were conducted from U.S. offices, and some foreign offices of U.S. banks were established for such purposes as the facilitation of trade, the marketing of American bonds, and the provision of assistance to Americans traveling in Europe.

Once the Federal Reserve Act of 1913 was passed, opening the door to foreign branching by national banks, a few banks responded quickly. Citibank (then, First National City Bank) opened its first foreign branch in Buenos Aires in 1914 and followed this with a number of other Latin American offices. Two ensuing legislative actions, the Federal Reserve Act amendment of 1916 (section 25) and addition (section 25[a]) of 1919 (the so-called "Edge Act"), contributed substantially to the powers of commercial banks to conduct their foreign business. The amendment of 1916 permitted national banks to invest in state-chartered corporations engaged in international or foreign banking and operating under an agreement with the Federal Reserve Board ("agreement corporations"). The Edge Act permitted U.S. banks to operate overseas and to conduct there activities which they could not conduct in the United States, such as investment banking and underwriting securities. Nevertheless, this increased flexibility was not used very widely. A limited number of banks opened branches, mostly in the less developed countries of Latin America and Asia, where American investment was growing and where the development of local banking lagged far behind that of Europe. During this early period, indications are that the involvement of U.S. banks in international activities was closely related to the levels of world trade and investment.[24] When trade and investment expanded during the 1920s, U.S. banks picked up a parallel trend and expanded abroad. When world depression stalled international trade and investment, there was a corresponding contraction in the foreign expansion of U.S. banks.

  Although major coastal U.S. banks have had branches abroad since the 1910s,[25] the period since 1960 marks the real beginning of multinational banking by U.S. banks. A network of correspondent relationships with banks in foreign countries and direct overseas lending from the head offices to foreign borrowers were the predominant multinational involvement of most U.S. banks before 1960. The ensuing boom in the establishment of foreign branches and subsidiaries was concomitant with the rapid expansion of U.S. multinational corporations around the world. With the global expansion of their clients, domestic banks attempted to match their clients' new needs, and began to set up branches and subsidiaries in the major and emerging financial centers of the world. Table 2-10 shows the evolutionary trends in foreign expansion of U.S. banks. As can be seen from the table, the heyday of U.S. multinational banking really began during the 1970s. However, the number of U.S. banks involved is somewhat misleading: still the vast majority of multinational operations of U.S. banks have been done by a small group of the largest banks.

  It has been indicated that a number of factors have influenced and facilitated the multinationalization of U.S. banks.[26] These were (1) the growth of U.S. foreign trade and foreign direct investment; (2) the advent of the Eurodollar market; (3) the U.S. balance of payments deficits and the ensuing restrictive regulations on capital outflow; (4) the heavy domestic loan demand and the tight credit policies of the U.S. during 1966 and 1969-70; and (5) the

## Table 2-10.    Foreign Branches of U.S. Banks

|  | U.S. Banks with Branches | Number of Branches | Total Assets of Overseas Branches (In Billions of Dollars) | Total Assets of All U.S. Commercial Banks (In Billions of Dollars) |
|---|---|---|---|---|
| 1960 | 8 | 131 | 3.5 | 255.7 |
| 1964 | 11 | 181 | 6.9 | 343.9 |
| 1965 | 13 | 211 | 9.1 | 374.1 |
| 1966 | 13 | 244 | 12.4 | 401.4 |
| 1967 | 15 | 295 | 15.7 | 448.9 |
| 1968 | 26 | 375 | 23.0 | 498.1 |
| 1969 | 53 | 459 | 41.1 | 527.6 |
| 1970 | 79 | 536 | 52.6 | 576.2 |
| 1971 | 91 | 583 | 67.1 | 640.3 |
| 1972 | 108 | 627 | 77.4 | 732.5 |
| 1973 | 122 | 699 | 118.0 | 827.1 |
| 1974 | 125 | 734 | 151.9 | 919.5 |
| 1975 | 126 | 762 | 176.5 | 964.9 |
| 1976 | 127 | 731 | 219.4 | 1,030.7 |
| 1977 | 124 | 730 | 258.9 | 1,166.0 |
| 1978 | 137 | 761 | 306.8 | 1,303.9 |
| 1979 | 139 | 789 | 364.2 | 1,351.0 |
| 1980 | 143 | 787 | 401.1 | 1,537.0 |
| 1981 | 151 | 841 | 462.6 | 1,653.7 |
| 1982 | 162 | 900 | 469.2 | 1,820.0 |

Note:   Figures may vary slightly depending on sources.

Sources:   First two columns: Treasury Forms B-2 and B-3 and Federal Reserve Board, listed in Brimmer and Dahl, "Growth of American International Banking: Implications for Public Policy," *The Journal of Finance,* May 1975, p. 345, Board of Governors of the Federal Reserve System, listed in Korth, "The Evolving Role of U.S. Banks in International Finance," *The Bankers Magazine,* July-Aug. 1981, p. 69; and *Federal Reserve Statistical Release,* various issues.

Third and fourth columns: Brimmer and Dahl, ibid, p. 345, Fieleke, "The Growth of U.S. Banking Abroad: An Analytical Survey," in *Key Issues in International Banking* (Federal Reserve Bank of Boston, Oct. 1977), p. 11 and *Federal Reserve Bulletin,* various issues.

permission to establish "shell" branches. However, in the case of non-U.S. MNBs, different motivating factors are also found. One survey[27] shows that the attractiveness of the host market and the importance of the host currency (i.e., U.S. dollar) for international transactions are important motivations of non-U.S. MNBs' expansion into the U.S. market, along with the need to finance home country trade with and direct investment in the U.S. (table 2-11).

Since each of these factors influenced differently the overseas expansion of banks at different times, the evolutionary patterns of the growth of U.S. MNBs can be categorized by the primary motivation for their multinational involvement. The remainder of this section will trace these patterns and investigate U.S. MNBs' multinational strategies since World War II.[28]

*Initial Expansion (Before 1958)*

U.S. international banking activities gradually gained importance following the emergence of the United States in the postwar period as the dominant economic and financial power in the world economy. The world economic environment of this period, characterized by increased opportunities for U.S. firms to participate in the economic recovery efforts in Western Europe, the progressive dismantling of barriers to international trade and capital movements, and the stable growth of the world economy since about 1950, helped to create opportunities for trade, investment, and lending on an international scale.

More direct impetus to the development of the international operations of U.S. banks was provided by the upsurge of direct investment abroad by U.S. corporations since the early 1950s. Corporations venturing into or expanding their international operations turned to their banks for financial assistance and for advice and information on the foreign markets in which they were interested. As U.S. business became more internationally oriented, it became necessary for major banks to establish international offices to serve their customers better and to fill the new demands of U.S. MNCs, whose banks at home could not adequately provide necessary international financial services. This period laid the groundwork for much of the subsequent expansion in the international operations of the major banks, and began the momentum which caused other banks to venture into international operations for fear of losing their customers. Profit opportunities motivated the initial expansion of U.S. banks. In addition, in the same manner as for their manufacturing counterparts, the banks' concern with continued growth, risk diversification, and stable client relationships abroad as well as at home must have influenced their international expansion. The fear of the consequences if they failed to follow their customers abroad appears to have loomed significantly in the calculations of banks whose large corporate customers went abroad. The fear of losing their multinational customers to foreign banks or other, more internationally active rival U.S. banks appears to have been a compelling factor in making banks go abroad to follow their customers.[29] As these banks perceived it, the failure to do so would threaten the earnings from the remaining business with the multinational customers both at home and abroad. It is this line of reasoning that can explain why the banks which were active in serving U.S. multinational corporations were the ones that were most seriously engaged in international operations.

Nevertheless, as table 2-12 shows, growth was sluggish throughout the postwar period until the late 1950s. Consequently, as a broad generalization, it is fair to characterize the international operations of American banks up to the mid-1950s as essentially passive, comprising mainly a service operation related

Table 2-11. Major Motivations of Non-US MNBs in the U.S. Market

Question: What motivated your decision to establish an operation in the U.S. market?

| Answers | Country of Origin | | | | | | | | | | |
|---|---|---|---|---|---|---|---|---|---|---|---|
| | Holland | Brazil | Argentina | England | France | Italy | Pakistan | Korea | Japan | Switzerland | Canada |
| Trade financing | x | *x | *x | x | x | | x | *x | *x | | *x |
| To stimulate home country market, attract business to it | | | | | | | | | | | |
| Competitive reasons (other home banks were here) | | | | | | | | | | | x |
| To service home trade and industrial companies financial needs | x | x | x | x | x | x | x | x | x | | x |
| Close political ties with the U.S. and stability of the U.S. economy | *x | | | | | | | x | x | x | x |
| To facilitate the operation of the network | | x | | | | | *x | | | x | x |
| Size of U.S. economy – room for everybody | x | | | x | x | x | | | | x | |
| Nature of the American market – receptivity to foreigners – less structure | | | | | | | | | | | |

## Table 2-11 (continued)

| Question: What motivated your decision to establish an operation in the U.S. market? | Country of Origin | | | | | | | | | | |
|---|---|---|---|---|---|---|---|---|---|---|---|
| Answers | Holland | Brazil | Argentina | England | France | Italy | Pakistan | Korea | Japan | Switzerland | Canada |
| To satisfy existing demand of large U.S. corporation for funds and participate in syndicated loans | x | x | | | x | x* | | | x | | x |
| Absence of controls on exchange transactions | | | | | | | x | | | | |
| Requested to by home trade companies | | | | | | | | x | x | | |
| Foreign exchange transactions – Importance of dollar | x | | | | x | | x | | | x | x |
| Number of their nationals in the United States, specifically in the market in which they opened | | x | | | | | | x* | | | |
| Closed markets elsewhere – rise of nationalism in former colonies | | | | x | | | | | | | |
| Technical advantages – must be in the U.S. market to properly assess risk and increase information flow – also get better rates and quantity to funds | x | x | x | | x | x | | | | | |
| They want the business instead of giving it to U.S. banks as it is profitable | | | | x | | | x* | | | | |

*Refers to the strength (high) of the motivation.

Source: Khoury (1980), p. 153.

Table 2-12.   Growth of Foreign Branch Networks of U.S. Banks

| | Number of banks | England | Europe | Latin America | Near East | Far East | U.S.A. Overseas Areas | Africa | Total Branches |
|---|---|---|---|---|---|---|---|---|---|
| 1953 | 7 | 10 | 7 | 54 | - | 20 | 14 | - | 105 |
| 1954 | 7 | 11 | 6 | 55 | - | 20 | 14 | - | 106 |
| 1955 | 7 | 11 | 6 | 56 | 4 | 20 | 14 | - | 111 |
| 1956 | 7 | 11 | 5 | 58 | 4 | 20 | 17 | - | 115 |
| 1957 | 7 | 11 | 5 | 60 | 4 | 20 | 17 | - | 117 |
| 1958 | 7 | 10 | 5 | 62 | 4 | 20 | 18 | - | 119 |
| 1959 | 7 | 10 | 5 | 69 | 4 | 20 | 22 | - | 132 |
| 1960 | 8 | 13 | 6 | 55[1] | 4 | 22 | 22 | - | 124[3] |
| 1961 | 8 | 13 | 6 | 62 | 3[2] | 22 | 23 | 1 | 135 |
| 1962 | 10 | 14 | 9 | 66 | 3 | 23 | 23 | 3 | 145 |
| 1963 | 10 | 14 | 12 | 73 | 4 | 23 | 23 | 3 | 160 |
| 1964 | 11 | 17 | 15 | 77 | 5 | 23 | 23 | 3 | 180[4] |
| 1965 | 13 | 24 | 22 | 88 | 5 | 23 | 23 | 2 | 211 |

1) 21 branches nationalized by Cuba in 1960

2) Branch in Cairo discontinued

3) "131" in Table II-10

4) "181" in Table II-10

Source:   Robin Pingle, "Why American Banks Go Overseas," The Banker (Nov. 1966), p. 772.

to the financing of U.S. foreign trade[30] and concentrating geographically in Latin America.

*Defensive Expansion (1959-1963)*

Once the first wave of foreign expansion which had brought major East Coast banks and a California bank[31] to overseas markets had passed, the second wave of multinationalization reached the U.S. banking industry. This period saw several developments which facilitated the expansion of U.S. banks abroad. They were (1) the gradual liberalization of foreign exchange control and capital movement by developed countries, (2) a return to convertibilities of major European currencies for current account transactions, (3) the lowering of trade barriers, (4) the formation of the European Common Market, and (5) the development of the Eurodollar market. Three new U.S. banks established their foreign branches during this period, while the banks already established abroad increased their overseas involvement. One New York bank (the Chemical Bank New York Trust Co. [1960]) and one Chicago bank (the Continental Illinois National Bank and Trust Co. of Chicago [1962]) established their branches in London, thus making the number of major U.S. commercial banks with branches in Europe nine by the end of the first Eurodollar operating phase.

Referring to the reasons for these banks' decisions to establish branches in London, Robinson reasons that "the Eurodollar market per se was not the primary reason to establish branch banks in the host countries (U.K., France, and Switzerland), although it did represent a significant element in an evolution which these institutions could not ignore. The principal reason for the establishment of the second wave branch banks was to serve directly their customers located in or near the host countries in order to compete effectively with the first wave branch banks already established. In effect, this was an attempt to bridge the widening gap in various banks' direct overseas experience. Those major U.S. banks not already established in the host countries were forced to decide whether they were ready to follow their clients and competitors onto the Western European stage of operations."[32]

This investment phenomenon seems to fit into Knickerbocker's "oligopolistic reaction" investment pattern. Knickerbocker explains the pattern of foreign direct investment activities of U.S. MNCs in Europe during the 1960s with an oligopoly model, suggesting that oligopolists follow each other into new foreign markets as a defensive strategy.[33] He reasons that once initiating firms establish production facilities in foreign markets, the other firms follow suit to negate any advantages that the former might gain, out of fear that the advantages acquired may threaten market positions within the industry. This oligopoly model helps explain the foreign investment decisions of MNCs in some industries where a small number of firms have led the way to overseas markets.

The Chemical Bank New York Trust Co. case fits well into this defensive investment pattern, in the sense that its major rival New York banks had already established themselves in serving U.S. MNCs for their international needs and, thus, a failure to match this would have meant a potential loss of its client MNCs' banking business overseas as well as at home. The Continental Illinois National Bank case also fits this model. Although it does not seem that the Continental Illinois and New York banks competed directly for their non-MNC clients (because their markets were separated), they must have competed with each other directly for their MNC clients. Thus, a failure by Continental Illinois to serve its MNC clients at least as adequately as its rival New York banks with already established branches overseas would have meant a drain of its MNC banking business and a decline of its market position in the industry.

When so many of their important clients were venturing into overseas operations, staying out would have presented risks too great for banks to bear—both actual and potential. When one of the major regional bank's competitors set up a branch or an affiliate in a country where the bank's major MNC customer was operating, the rival so established was in a favorable position to get the customer's subsidiary's banking business. The risk of losing business was not confined to a single country or a single subsidiary. Chances were that the MNC client, having established satisfactory relations with the rival bank in a specific market, might turn to the same bank for its banking business in other markets. The widening circle of banks engaged seriously in multinational banking during this period seems to be a sign of these competitive forces at work. We can find this trend continued throughout the next waves of expansion with greater or lesser intensity.

One notable characteristic of this period is that whereas a California bank (Bank of America) had been the sole non-New York City bank among those with first wave branches in Europe, by the end of the first Eurodollar operating phase non-New York City banks accounted for two of the eight. This reflected the rising multinational aspirations of bankers in other parts of the United States, which became intensified in later periods.

*Offshore Banking Boom (1964-1974)*

The period from 1964 through 1974 marks a peak of international expansion by U.S. banks. It was mainly prompted by: (1) the continued increase in U.S. foreign trade and foreign direct investment, (2) the proliferation of the Eurodollar market, (3) U.S. government regulations aimed at improving U.S. balance of payments, (4) U.S. tight money policies in 1966 and 1969-70, and (5) the permission for "shell" branches.[34]

The U.S. balance of payments policies from 1964 to early 1974 were instrumental in prompting the development of the Eurodollar market and, thus, the multinational expansion of U.S. banks. Three measures were taken to improve the U.S. balance of payments: (1) the Interest Equalization Tax (IET) Act, passed in 1964, designed to discourage foreigners' access to U.S. capital markets by reducing the effective yield on foreign bonds issued in the U.S.; (2) the Voluntary Foreign Credit Restraint Program (VFCR), passed in 1965 and becoming mandatory in 1968, designed to curtail the foreign lending of U.S. commercial banks; and (3) the Foreign Direct Investment Program (FDIP), designed to limit U.S. corporations' ability to transfer funds overseas for direct investment.

Although these laws and regulations were ineffective in reducing the balance of payments deficits, they were said to be very effective in encouraging U.S. banks to locate overseas.[35] At the end of 1964, as shown in table 2-12, only eleven banks had established branches abroad—although in combination those eleven banks were operating from 181 foreign locations. By the end of 1974, there were 125 banks with a total of 734 foreign branches (table 2-10). These controls effectively moved the foreign lending activities away from the U.S. parent banks to their foreign branches, especially those located in London and later to branches in the Bahamas. At the end of 1973, nearly 90 percent of U.S. banks' total foreign credits outstanding were on the books of their foreign branches.[36]

During this period, most of the growth of U.S. commercial bank branches had centered primarily in offshore financial markets—London, the Bahamas and the Cayman Islands—to obtain access to the Eurodollar market (table 2-13). This was mainly due to (1) the need for an overseas office that could deal directly with U.S. multinational customers to raise funds abroad in compliance with the U.S. government's balance of payments policies, and (2) the need for a "window" for taking Eurodollar deposits that could be used for lending to these borrowers and, ultimately, to channel funds to its head office in the U.S. to enable the latter to cushion the impact of domestic monetary restraint.[37] Later, a number of banks (including some of the largest in the country) opened Nassau shell branches primarily for the purpose of benefiting from the favorable tax laws of the Bahamas.[38]

Since the U.S. banks' clients (mainly MNCs) were expanding overseas greatly during this period, part of the banks' multinational expansion was motivated by a desire to serve the clients overseas. This expansion was enhanced by the restraints on capital outflow imposed on U.S. direct investors by the U.S. Department of Commerce.[39] By lending from their foreign branches, and therefore outside the VFCR, U.S. commercial banks could assist their customers to comply with the restraints on financing foreign investment with U.S.-source funds.

Table 2-13. Overseas Branches of U.S. Member Banks, 1965 to 1975 (As of January 1, 1975)

| Country of location | 1965 | 1966 | 1967 | 1968 | 1969 | 1970 | 1971 | 1972 | 1973 | 1974 | 1975 |
|---|---|---|---|---|---|---|---|---|---|---|---|
| Belgium-Luxembourg | 2 | 4 | 6 | 8 | 9 | 11 | 11 | 8 | 8 | 15 | 15 |
| France | 4 | 4 | 4 | 6 | 7 | 11 | 12 | 15 | 17 | 15 | 17 |
| German | 3 | 6 | 8 | 9 | 14 | 17 | 21 | 22 | 27 | 30 | 30 |
| Greece | 1 | 1 | 1 | 2 | 5 | 8 | 9 | 13 | 14 | 16 | 18 |
| Italy | 1 | 1 | 1 | 2 | 2 | 3 | 4 | 6 | 7 | 8 | 10 |
| Netherlands | 3 | 3 | 3 | 3 | 5 | 7 | 7 | 7 | 6 | 6 | 6 |
| Switzerland | 1 | 1 | 2 | 3 | 3 | 6 | 7 | 8 | 8 | 9 | 9 |
| United Kingdom | 17 | 21 | 21 | 24 | 32 | 37 | 41 | 45 | 49 | 52 | 55 |
| Total Europe | 32 | 43 | 48 | 59 | 80 | 103 | 116 | 128 | 142 | 157 | 167 |
| Bahamas | 2 | 3 | 3 | 3 | 8 | 32 | 60 | 73 | 94 | 91 | 80 |
| Cayman Islands | | | | | | | | | 2 | 32 | 44 |
| Total Caribbean[2] | 5 | 9 | 9 | 10 | 22 | 53 | 89 | 105 | 133 | 165 | 166 |
| Argentina | 16 | 17 | 17 | 25 | 33 | 38 | 38 | 38 | 38 | 38 | 37 |
| Brazil | 15 | 15 | 15 | 15 | 15 | 15 | 16 | 19 | 21 | 21 | 19 |
| Colombia | 5 | 6 | 6 | 8 | 17 | 23 | 26 | 28 | 28 | 32 | 36 |
| Panama | 10 | 12 | 15 | 19 | 21 | 26 | 29 | 29 | 32 | 33 | 33 |
| Total Latin America[3] | 78 | 88 | 102 | 133 | 177 | 235 | 281 | 296 | 322 | 356 | 363 |

[1] Also includes Austria, Ireland, Monaco, and Romania.
[2] Also includes Barbados, Haiti, Jamaica, Netherlands Antilles, Trinidad and Tobago, British Virgin Islands, and other West Indies.

Table 2-13 (continued)

| Country of location | 1965 | 1966 | 1967 | 1968 | 1969 | 1970 | 1971 | 1972 | 1973 | 1974 | 1975 |
|---|---|---|---|---|---|---|---|---|---|---|---|
| China, Republic of Taiwan | | | 2 | 2 | 2 | 2 | 2 | 2 | 3 | 5 | 7 |
| Hong Kong | 6 | 6 | 8 | 10 | 12 | 13 | 13 | 15 | 19 | 23 | 24 |
| India | 5 | 6 | 8 | 8 | 11 | 11 | 11 | 11 | 11 | 11 | 11 |
| Indonesia | | | | | 4 | 6 | 6 | 6 | 6 | 6 | 6 |
| Japan | 13 | 14 | 14 | 14 | 14 | 15 | 15 | 17 | 21 | 25 | 31 |
| Lebanon | 3 | 3 | 3 | 3 | 3 | 3 | 3 | 3 | 3 | 3 | 3 |
| Persian Gulf[4] | 2 | 2 | 3 | 3 | 3 | 3 | 8 | 11 | 10 | 10 | 11 |
| Singapore | 8 | 8 | 8 | 8 | 8 | 9 | 11 | 11 | 11 | 14 | 18 |
| Total Asia[5] | 45 | 55 | 63 | 69 | 78 | 83 | 90 | 97 | 109 | 122 | 138 |
| Total Africa[6] | 3 | 2 | 2 | 3 | 3 | 1 | 2 | 2 | 2 | 2 | 5 |
| Overseas areas of United States | 23 | 23 | 29 | 31 | 35 | 37 | 40 | 44 | 47 | 52 | 53 |
| Grand total | 180 | 211 | 244 | 295 | 373 | 460 | 532 | 577 | 627 | 699 | 732 |
| U.S. member banks with overseas branches | 11 | 13 | 13 | 15 | 26 | 53 | 79 | 91 | 107 | 125 | 125 |

[3] Also includes Bolivia, Chile, [*]Dominican Republic, Ecuador, El Salvador, Guatemala, Guyana, Honduras, Mexico, Paraguay, Peru, Uruguay, and Venezuela.

[4] Includes Bahrain, Qatar, Saudi Arabia, and United Arab Emirates.

[5] Also includes Brunei, Israel, Korea, Malaysia, Pakistan, Philippines, Thailand, and Vietnam.

[6] Includes Liberia, Kenya, Mauritius, and Nigeria.[*]

[*] No resident U.S. branches as of January 1, 1975.

Source: Federal Reserve Bank of Chicago, listed in Sarkis J. Khoury, Dynamics of International Banking (New York: Praeger Publishers, 1980), pp. 42–3.

*Realignment (Since 1975)*

The U.S. banks have ceased the rapid creation of foreign branches since 1975. One reason was the dismantling of controls on capital flows, which permitted more lending from home offices. In addition, many banks by this time found that international banking required skills which they did not have, and many found that the costs were higher and the profits lower than expected.[40] But the more important reason may be the existence of obstacles to the growth of U.S. banks' total assets in general and their international asset expansion in particular.

Traditionally, banks tend to determine their deposit-taking and lending activities by considering the outlook for profit opportunities and the expected evolution of the banks' capital base. Since 1975, U.S. banks—especially the largest—have faced two major domestic challenges: the growth of nonbank financial intermediation (especially via the commercial paper market) and the expansion of domestic lending from many foreign banks operating within the United States. Both challenges have reduced the market share held by U.S. banks for short- and medium-term corporate lending, and both have clouded the prospects of rapid or profitable expansion of domestic assets. Internationally, they have faced a very competitive market where numerous relatively less exposed, less supervised, and less experienced foreign financial institutions vie for the available business. This factor, together with the reasons mentioned above, can explain the slow pace of multinational expansion of U.S. banks since 1975.

The period has seen notable developments that have significantly influenced the multinational activities of U.S. banks, and in fact the banks of most other countries. The sharp increase in oil prices has created massive trade surpluses for oil-exporting nations along with large deficits for the major oil-importing countries. This has necessitated a new role of recycling surpluses of oil-exporting nations to the deficit oil-importing nations by multinational commercial banks—especially U.S. commercial banks. The consequent changes of the international banking market into a borrower's market, mainly due to an excess supply of loanable funds by OPEC nations, recession in developed countries, relatively few creditworthy borrowers (mostly several LDCs and their government agencies), and increased competition among existing multinational banks (mostly large U.S. banks) and from new entrants of other developed countries (notably, Japan and West Germany), squeezed profitability on wholesale banking in the Eurodollar market—the main activity carried on by U.S. branch banks (tables 2-8, 2-14). In 1976, for example, the return on domestic assets averaged 0.40 percent for the ten most internationally active American banks while the return on international assets was 0.52

Table 2-14.  International Earnings of Ten Largest U.S. Commercial
Banks (As % of Total Earnings)

|  | 1975 | 1976 | 1977 | 1978 | 1979 | 1980 | 1981 | 1982 | 1983 |
|---|---|---|---|---|---|---|---|---|---|
| Citicorp | 71% | 72% | 80% | 72% | 65% | 62% | 65% | 63% | 54% |
| Bank of America | 55% | 47% | 42% | 35% | 38% | 45% | 63% | 63% | 47% |
| Chase Manhattan | 64% | 78% | 65% | 53% | 47% | 49% | 60% | 70% | 42% |
| Manufacturers Hanover | 47% | 59% | 60% | 51% | 49% | 57% | 51% | 50% | 49% |
| J.P. Morgan | 60% | 46% | 48% | 51% | 52% | 72% | 73% | 72% | 54% |
| Chemical New York | 41% | 41% | 39% | 42% | 35% | 36% | 36% | 43% | 42% |
| Bankers Trust New York | 59% | 61% | 83% | 68% | 51% | 63% | 62% | 47% | 39% |
| Continental Illinois | 14% | 23% | 17% | 18% | 18% | 32% | 29% | 66% | 7% |
| First Chicago | 33% | 15% | 20% | 16% | 44% | -37% | 17% | 29% | 12% |
| Security Pacific | 12% | 7% | 12% | 15% | 10% | 14% | 25% | 32% | 17% |
| Weighted Average | 52% | 51% | 51% | 46% | 43% | 51% | 54% | 58% | 42% |

Sources:   Salomon Brothers, listed in Arturo C. Porzecanski, "The International Financial Role of U.S. Commercial Banks:
Past and Future," *Journal of Banking and Finance,* 5 (1981), p. 10.
Individual banks' *annual reports and 10-K reports.*

percent. Since that time, however, falling spreads on loans to virtually all
foreign borrowers have helped to reverse the banks' profit picture, with returns
on international assets dropping gradually to 0.44 percent in 1979 and 0.51
percent in 1983. Consequently, the contribution of international earnings to
total bank earnings declined from 52 percent in 1975 to 43 percent in 1979 and
42 percent in 1983. During the period from 1976 to 1983, the international
earnings of the ten largest U.S. banks increased by about 10 percent per annum
(versus 20 percent per annum during the period from 1973 to 1976) which
contrasts with domestic earnings growth of approximately 14 percent per
year.[41] Recent repayment problems of major sovereign borrowers of U.S.
MNBs—especially Mexico, Argentina, Brazil, and Venezuela—have further
squeezed their international earnings as they need to strengthen their loan loss
reserves for potential problem sovereign loans.

Faced with increased competition in both domestic markets and
traditional international banking markets, and increased risk exposure in their
sovereign lending market, U.S. banks began to think of international product
diversification.[42] International product diversification was also influenced by
some changes in U.S. banking regulations. Other than the 1960 and 1966
amendments to the Edge Act, which permitted U.S. banks wider latitude in
their international banking activities, the 1970 amendments to the Bank

Holding Company Act removed the distinction between a one-bank holding company and a multibank holding company and enabled banks to diversify into nonbanking businesses through a general purpose holding company.

With limited growth prospects at home and increased competition abroad (especially in the traditional banking activities of wholesale lending), U.S. banks have moved to diversify from retail banking to a complete package of financial services, such as merchant banking and equity financing. They also have diversified geographically. An increasing number have moved into less developed markets, notably Asia and Latin America.

In sum, the multinationalization process of U.S. banks has been quite complex. No single explanation can rightly characterize the evolutionary patterns of multinationalization of U.S. banks. However, the overview shows that a few identifiable changes in market opportunities have been stronger than others in prompting the multinational involvement of U.S. banks.

# 3

# Theories on Multinational Banking and Multinational Banks

The postwar pattern of multinational expansion in the banking industry has attracted relatively less systematic attention than that of the manufacturing and extractive industries, though the multinationalization phenomenon in banking is similarly impressive. Most studies on multinational banking have concentrated on the mechanisms of Eurocurrency markets, the functional aspects of multinational banking, or the applicability of the general theories of MNCs to the banking industry. Only recently have several attempts been made to explain the why, how, and where of the multinationalization phenomenon in the banking industry.

Generally, a bank can be involved in international operations in a number of ways, as explained in chapter 2. The simplest method is through correspondent banking relationships. A correspondent relation acts as a kind of sales agency for the bank which wishes to engage in international banking activities. This is the equivalent of the exporting activities of manufacturing firms. Another type of international involvement is through the establishment of overseas offices. This method can take various organizational forms—a representative office, an agency, a branch, a joint venture, or a majority-owned subsidiary. This is the equivalent of the foreign direct investment (FDI) activities of manufacturing firms. Regardless of the specific organizational form, this type of involvement implies the transfer of capital, managerial, and technological assets of a bank from one country to another by the same bank. Another possible means of international involvement would be through the licensing agreement.[1] But, although this type of involvement is prevalent in certain service industries such as the hotel industry and the advertising industry, there seem to be few licensing agreements in banking. This may be due to certain unique characteristics of the banking industry—absence of an extensive patent system, ease of product imitation, and limited product differentiability. Thus, it can be said that a correspondent relation and an overseas office are the two major types of international involvement in the banking industry. The major difference between them is that a correspondent relationship is not accompanied by control over the transferred assets (investment). Therefore, to explain properly the FDI phenomenon in the banking industry, the following questions should be answered simultaneously: (1) what advantages does a bank have which allow it to compete against local and/or other foreign banks? (2) why is a foreign rather than a domestic operation advantageous in serving foreign and/or domestic markets? and (3) why does a bank choose to exploit these advantages itself rather than selling them to local and/or other foreign banks?

Most of the theories regarding multinational banks have developed along the paths attempting to answer these questions. Each is, however, only a partial explanation of FDI in the banking industry, as each answers only one or two strands of these questions. In this chapter, existing theories on multinational banking will be reviewed on the basis of the underlying disciplines employed and the need for a new approach will be emphasized.

## Comparative Advantage Theory

One set of hypotheses about the multinationalization of banks is based on theories of comparative advantage (Lees, 1974; Aliber, 1976). It is argued that "[international] banking will be most substantial in those countries which have a comparative advantage in producing bank products. . . ."[2] Aliber (1976) sees the persistence of large differences in loan-deposit spreads across countries as a major cause of multinational banking and argues such differences are caused by different comparative advantages of a bank in producing banking products. He contends that the comparative advantages in producing certain banking products arise from the efficiency of banks and from the different national regulations on the costs of producing them. Aliber argues that free trade in money would eliminate any observed differences in spreads across countries, but the existence of "barriers to trade" in money, mostly caused by different national regulations, creates such differences which reflect the underlying efficiency of each country's banks. Thus, a bank with comparative advantages in producing certain banking products needed in foreign markets is believed to be most likely to serve the foreign markets.

However, the wider spreads could occur due to government-mandated externalities which might not have any bearing on a bank's efficiency. Furthermore, utilization of these advantages may not necessarily require a physical banking presence in foreign markets, which accompanies a cross-border movement of capital, managerial, and technological resources. They can be successfully exploited through cross-border transactions at the home office. Comparative advantage theory explains who should produce a certain banking product and where it should be sold, but it does not explain where and how that product should be produced. It does not provide any insight on the sources of these comparative advantages and why a bank would want to exploit them by itself.

**Industrial Organization Theory**

Another set of hypotheses about the multinationalization of banks is based on industrial organization theories (Goldberg, 1973; Brimmer and Dahl, 1975; Aliber, 1976; Grubel, 1977; Fieleke, 1977; Allen and Giddy, 1979; Khoury, 1980; Goldberg and Saunders, 1981). Aliber (1976) also contends that banks based in countries with high concentration ratios would be more profitable— and thus better able to satisfy capital expansion needs (for international banking) due to the higher loan-deposit spreads in the domestic market—than those in countries with lower concentration ratios.[3] He sees the comparative advantage theory and the industrial organization theory as complementary ways of viewing the phenomenon of multinational banking and regards the existence of different spreads as a result of different competitive situations across countries. However, banks can raise funds (for their international expansion) in external capital markets, and it is not unambiguously clear that internal funds are always cheaper. Furthermore, much empirical evidence to the contrary can be found. In fact, some banks based in countries with low concentration ratios go abroad to avoid competitive pressures in home countries or to strengthen their market positions in home countries. Singapore and Hong Kong banks provide a good example.

Grubel (1977) puts forward a three-stream theory providing alternate explanations for the development of multinational retail banking, multinational service banking and multinational wholesale banking. He contends that the existence of different kinds of surplus entrepreneurial resources (such as management technology, organization and marketing know-how and commercial intelligence) is instrumental in facilitating multinationalization in retail and service banking, whereas imperfections in the international capital markets explain the development of multinational wholesale banking. Grubel's theoretical explanation is identical to the explanations of Hymer (1960/1976), Kindleberger (1969), and Caves (1971). But the mere possession of surplus entrepreneurial resources would not provide a convincing explanation of multinational banking unless the way these resources are combined with other resources is explained.

Brimmer and Dahl (1975), Fieleke (1977), Khoury (1980), and Goldberg and Saunders (1981), among others, explain the postwar pattern of growth of multinational banking as a response of MNBs to the multinationalization and geographical diversification of the operations of their home country customers. They reason that such defensive measures are necessary to assure the continued business with the domestic parents of the foreign subsidiaries. Failure to accompany the subsidiaries abroad would, they argue, force them to turn to foreign banks or domestic rivals with branches abroad for deposits, loans, and other services and, eventually, such growing commercial relationships might expand to where domestic business is overtaken by local or foreign banking competitors. While certain elements of defensiveness are found among MNBs of earlier periods,[4] a major reason would be the fact that they can serve their home customers operating overseas on better terms than other foreign banks due to their cost advantages in the credit rating of their home customers (Goldberg, 1973, p. 90; Vastrup, 1983, p. 120). Furthermore, a major reason for relatively small banks, such as U.S. regional banks, to establish branch offices in offshore banking markets would not necessarily be a defensive one.

**International Investment Theory**

Various causes of imperfections in international financial markets are often cited as major underlying reasons for the existence of MNBs. Due to various externalities in the markets, which are caused by either government-imposed distortions, market structure imperfections, or market failures, a bank is expected to go overseas to avoid or exploit these externalities.

Brimmer and Dahl (1975) and Kelly (1977) contend that government regulations on capital flows were the major motivation of U.S. banks to expand into European markets during the sixties and early seventies. They reason that a series of U.S. government regulations[5] to restrict capital outflow motivated U.S. banks to go into the European markets to serve their customers' international financial needs. It cannot be denied that the U.S. government regulations of the sixties accelerated U.S. banks' expansion into the European markets. However, if that had been the cause of major significance, the removal of these restrictions should have shown a decrease of U.S. overseas banking activities or, at least, the growth of international banking activities would have been faster during the period of capital controls than in their absence. But the reality since early 1974 when these restrictions were removed has been quite the opposite. Furthermore, this argument seems meaningful only when a bank expands into offshore banking markets where regulations on banking markets are relatively less restrictive or nonexistent. It fails to explain adequately the phenomenon of banking expansion into foreign onshore markets where regulatory differences are insignificant or tend to be more restrictive toward foreign banks.

Another explanation based on imperfections in capital markets centers on a bank's efforts to reduce risk through foreign diversification of investments. Fieleke (1977) hypothesizes that as economic conditions do not change in one country in the same way or at the same time as in other countries, a multicountry diversification may reduce the variability of the overall profit rate. But his study employing U.S. banking performance in ten and eight countries, for the years 1974 and 1975, respectively, cannot provide a conclusive test of this hypothesis.

Overall, the international investment theory is helpful in explaining sources of location-related advantages of MNBs. It reasons that imperfections in international financial markets create location-related advantages (or disadvantages) for banks and that in the process of exploiting (or avoiding) them, MNBs come into existence. But one readily conceivable shortcoming of this explanation of MNBs is that avoidance and exploitation of market imperfections can be possible without necessarily transferring financial, technological, and managerial resources. It also cannot explain sufficiently the different multinationalization patterns among banks from the same country.

**Internalization Theory**

An attempt to apply the concept of internalization to explain the activities of international banks was first made by Rugman (1981).[6] Recognizing the existence of Coasian-type externalities[7] in international financial markets, he contends that multinational banks act as vehicles for the internalization of these imperfections. In the process of internalization, he argues, multinational banks can benefit more than domestic banks since internalization benefits in international financial markets are greater than those in domestic financial markets because of the greater size of imperfections in international markets, and multinational banks can enjoy benefits from the additional advantage of international diversification. Furthermore, he argues that "the potential advantages of international banking are probably greater than those of international production and sales by the multinational firm due to the additional costs of operating in foreign factor and goods markets, costs which are incurred by the multinational enterprise by virtue of its role as a producer, but costs which are avoided by the multinational bank since its involvement in foreign nations is confined to the provision of financial services."[8]

Overall, Rugman's realization of the process of internalization as one of the essential characteristics of multinational banks seems to be a valuable contribution toward explaining the phenomenon of MNBs. This explains why a bank takes the form of a branch or subsidiary to service foreign markets rather than undertaking international intermediation through correspondent connections. An MNB decides to exploit its ownership advantages within its own system instead of contracting them in a regular market which, with its various imperfections, cannot price them adequately.

However, Rugman's explanations seem to be insufficient to be called a "general theory"[9] for several reasons. First, his model fails to explain the sources of ownership-specific advantages of an MNB which are to be internalized. Without addressing this, one cannot explain the existence of different degrees of multinationalization among banks from the same country. According to Rugman's reasoning, banks from the same country are supposed to have equal chances of multinationalization in a certain foreign market. Second, his model does not explain why an MNB selects a particular market over others for its multinational banking activities. The mere existence of imperfections in a certain financial market does not necessarily provide any incentives for a bank to establish a branch/subsidiary there. Only when conditions in a certain foreign market facilitate the exploitation of a bank's ownership advantages through internalization to a greater extent than do conditions in other foreign markets does a bank choose that market over others to launch its multinational banking activities. Thus, an important consideration for MNBs is not the mere existence of imperfections in certain foreign markets, but the different interactive effects of these imperfections with their ownership advantages. The relative attractiveness of the imperfections of a particular market vis-à-vis other markets is a deciding factor of choosing one market over others for MNBs' banking activities. Third, Rugman's model fails to recognize the possibilities of involvement of resources other than financial information in multinational banking. MNBs, like MNCs, require a joint transfer of financial, technological and managerial resources. International intermediation at home headquarters through correspondent connections involves a transfer of financial information alone—which, in the case of manufacturing firms, is equivalent to exporting, not foreign direct investment. Finally, Rugman's model cannot avoid a lack of dynamism which is one of the basic shortcomings of the internalization theory approach to explaining foreign direct investment in various industries.

## Eclectic Theory

Gray and Gray (1981) attempt to apply Dunning's eclectic theory of international production (Dunning, 1977, 1979, 1980) to multinational commercial banking. The eclectic theory stipulates three conditions of multinationality in terms of the existence of three kinds of advantages—ownership advantage, location advantage, and internalization advantage. The theory combines industrial organization theory, internalization theory, and location theory to explain the multinationalization of a firm. Gray and Gray note the appropriateness of the eclectic theory in explaining multinational banking and identify various imperfections in factor and product markets of multinational banking and location-related motivations of a MNB. However, they fail to investigate the importance of ownership-specific advantages and do not try to identify the sources of the objects of internalization. Yannopoulos (1983) refines this approach further and explores the three kinds of advantages essential for multinational banking. However, both studies fail to investigate the sources of advantages empirically and to test the eclectic model with actual experiences of MNBs. Nevertheless, the perceptions of Gray and Gray and Yannopoulos of the need for an eclectic approach in explaining multinational banking and MNBs are unique and valuable.

Conceptually, this approach is quite convincing in explaining the current foreign direct investment phenomenon in the banking industry though a categorization of particular advantages is not always unambiguous. The eclectic theory explains why foreign rather than domestic production is advantageous, what advantages a bank has which enable it to compete against local banks, and why it chooses to exploit these advantages itself rather than selling them to local banks.

The preceding examination of the various approaches toward explaining multinational banking and MNBs shows that only the eclectic theory can explain properly the three conditions outlined in chapter 2: (1) the advantages of MNBs, (2) where these advantages are exploited, and (3) how these advantages are exploited. The existence of proprietary advantages as such fails to provide a convincing theory on multinational banking unless one can explain where and how these advantages are exploited to enable multinational banking to be competitive. The benefits of internalization alone would not create MNBs unless banks have bank-specific advantages to be internalized and find overseas markets where these benefits can be maximized. Thus, there arises the need for an integrated approach which can shed light on the three conditions for multinational banking. Furthermore, it would be useful to have a unified theory which can explain and predict the emergence of different modes of multinational involvement in the banking industry as special cases of a more general model.

A theory of multinational banking should be able to explain the postwar pattern of development of multinational banking—such as, why some banks from a few countries have prevailed in the multinational banking scene, why some MNBs start at the wholesale end of the market while others start at the retail end, why MNBs take different forms of multinational involvement, why some MNBs try to escape market imperfections through offshore banking while others try to capitalize on imperfections in overseas markets through onshore banking. Furthermore, a theory of multinational banking should be able to explain the sources of MNBs' proprietary advantages. In this regard, the eclectic theory developed by Dunning seems to be useful. The eclectic theory would explain the patterns of multinationalization in the banking industry as the particular outcome of interactions among ownership-specific, location-specific, and internalization advantages of individual banks at a given time and in a given market.

In the following chapter, an integrated approach will be presented to identify the three conditions of multinational banking and MNBs within the context of the eclectic theory.

# 4

# Determinants of Growth of Multinational Banks: An Eclectic Model

The eclectic theory hypothesizes three conditions for multinationality of firms: (1) possession of net ownership advantages vis-à-vis firms of other nationalities; (2) existence of favorable comparative location-specific advantages in particular markets to be served; and (3) existence of incentives to internalize these advantages, rather than utilize them on a contractual basis. One way to ascertain the applicability of the eclectic theory to multinational banking is to specify the nature of ownership advantages required by MNBs, the nature of locational influences on banking, and the scope of internalization in multinational banking, and to study how different combinations of these conditions generate different degrees and types of involvement in multinational banking among MNBs and how these advantages are related to various kinds of MNB banking activity. This approach will be developed in this chapter.

## Nature of Determinants of MNBs

The eclectic theory stipulates three conditions of multinationality in terms of the existence of three kinds of advantage—ownership advantage, location advantage, and internalization advantage. In this section, the nature of these advantages and their relations with MNB activities will be examined.

### Ownership Advantages of MNBs

Ownership-specific advantages are those features which make a bank of one nation competitive with other banks in particular foreign markets including both indigenous and foreign banks. Ownership-specific advantages are a prerequisite to multinationalization. They should be sufficient to overcome the advantages which indigenous banks have in that market. Ownership-specific advantages largely take the form of intangible assets which are, at least for a period of time, specific to the bank possessing them. Access to skilled personnel and other managerial resources, access to favorable financial sources, possession of widespread and efficient networks, accumulated knowledge and experience in multinational operations, expertise in servicing the banking needs of particular customer groups (industries), and established creditworthiness in multinational banking circles are typical sources of ownership-specific advantages of MNBs.

One feature of ownership-specific advantages is a bank's ability to differentiate its banking products. Product differentiation can result from superior marketing techniques, research and development, accumulated commercial information on particular markets and customer groups, and a bank's prestige. As these resources are not available to all banks, at least not on favorable terms, a bank's ability to differentiate products can provide it with competitive advantages over others in particular markets. However, opportunities to create and to retain proprietary control over differentiated products are relatively limited in the banking industry. Due to a limited number of attributes of banking products[1] and the absence of a proper patent system, most products are easily imitated.[2] Furthermore, possibilities of innovation and creation of completely new products are extremely limited in the banking industry compared with the manufacturing industry.[3] Thus, advantages of product differentiation derived from research and development are comparatively scarce for MNBs. Instead, product differentiation via possession of valuable commercial information on particular markets and customer groups, retention of skilled personnel, and a bank's prestige is frequent in multinational banking. Project financing, syndicated loans, cofinancing, and sovereign lending are examples where such product differentiation is common.

A bank's ability to tap reliable sources of quality funds is another feature of ownership-specific advantages. In markets with relatively little potential for product differentiation, access to cheaper funds implies a significant competitive edge to the accessing bank. A bank's borrowing costs usually reflect the risk and return characteristics of its asset portfolios and its leverages. The size of a bank, its experience in multinational operations, the scope of its network and its reputation are largely responsible for its ability to secure funds. The size of a bank is usually closely related to its reputation; size represents reliability and stability to a bank's depositors and lenders, both realistically and perceptually. The wide banking network is essential to the development of extensive sources of deposits as deposit soliciting requires closer and frequent contacts with depositors. Nationality of a bank, which is a location-specific factor, is also related to this sourcing ability.[4] A bank's reputation is frequently found to be instrumental in soliciting quality deposits and borrowing funds in the interbank markets at lower rates.

Scale economies are also an important feature of ownership-specific advantages in multinational banking. Though one study shows the evidence of scale economies in banking is not strong (Mullineaux, 1978), a distinction between wholesale and retail banking might result in different findings. Possibilities of economies of scale are clearly found in the areas of wholesale lending, foreign exchange management, and international clearing services.

### Location Advantages of MNBs

Location-specific advantages are those benefits accruing to a certain location due to differences in location-specific endowments between countries. A bank can acquire these advantages simply by operating in that location. These advantages form a necessary, though not a sufficient, condition for the multinational operation of banks. Most location advantages are not bank-specific by themselves, but their combined effects with ownership-specific advantages and internalization advantages are bank-specific and differ among banks. Major sources of location-specific advantages can generally be found in five areas: different national regulatory frameworks, effective interest rate differentials, different economic situations, nationality of banks, and general socioeconomic differences.

Differences in tax systems, reserve requirements, foreign exchange regulations, banking systems, and scope of banking activities permitted are examples of national regulatory differences. Differences in banking regulations are a major contributing factor in the emergence of offshore banking (Dufey and Giddy, 1978). Different national regulatory requirements provide banks with offices in countries where the regulatory requirements are minimal with competitive edges over banks in other countries. Locations with minimal reserve requirements, a favorable tax system, and minimal official restrictions on pricing (interest rates), credit allocation, and capital flows will evidently give cost advantages to banks with offices in those locations, whether they be host or home countries, over banks in locations without them.

Effective interest rate differentials enable MNBs to acquire a significant location advantage. If international financial markets were efficient, there would be little possibility of effective interest rate differentials between national financial markets, due to financial arbitrage. But, in reality, international financial markets are relatively segmented and inefficient. Financial markets of most LDCs are relatively segmented from those of other countries and various imperfections are indicated among and within well-developed financial markets of developed countries.[5] Various government-imposed barriers and structural imperfections of the markets themselves make free functioning of international arbitrage difficult and, thus, create effective interest rate differentials between national financial markets. In a perfect market, any differences in interest rates between national financial markets are supposed to be offset by changes in exchange rates between national currencies. In the imperfect markets of reality, MNBs can capitalize on the existence of effective interest rate differentials by sourcing funds in lower interest rate markets and lending them in higher interest rate markets, which uninational indigenous banks cannot do competitively. This suggests the possibility of different effective interest rates among banks, depending on their portfolios of funding sources and lending outlets.

Differences in economic situation between countries create a potential for location advantages, too. Size of the economy, level of economic development, structure of the economy, home country economic presence in host markets, and availability of a pool of skilled personnel are examples of differentiating factors. Upgrading the structure of the economy, with higher dependence on the manufacturing sector for national production, generally requires a more active and advanced banking sector, which creates increased business opportunities for banks in the country. Increased trade between host and home countries and increased home country foreign direct investments in host countries may result in increased home country banking presence in host countries, as banks from home countries may have a better chance of serving the financial needs of home country firms than banks of other countries, including host country banks. This is largely due to the fact that either home country banks already have had significant banking relations with the investing firms, or they can acquire relevant commercial information on them at relatively lower costs.

Nationality of banks can generate a considerable competitive edge for banks from particular countries. Banks from vehicle currency countries acquire an advantage over banks from nonvehicle currency countries in dealing with transactions denominated in their home currencies, as such transactions incur lower transaction costs. They do not incur risks and costs involved in foreign exchange management. Furthermore, those banks have additional advantages of easier access to the sources of vehicle currencies, which nonvehicle currency banks may not acquire competitively. The dominant role of the U.S. dollar in international payments, and the need to clear dollar-denominated transactions through clearing facilities in New York, present U.S. banks with distinct advantages over banks with nondollar fund sources. Nationality is also related to a bank's trade name and creditworthiness, which is a source of ownership-specific advantages.

Finally, general sociocultural differences create other possibilities of location-specific advantages. Similarities in social system, business culture, and language can reduce costs of communication and adaptation in host countries.

*Internalization Advantages of MNBs*

Internalization advantages refer to the kinds of benefit a bank acquires when it chooses to form internal markets within the hierarchy instead of relying on arm's length external market channels to exploit its ownership-specific advantages. These advantages arise largely because of imperfections and failures in both factor and goods markets. Banks use information extensively as an intermediate input in supplying banking services, and the markets for information are characterized by important imperfections.[6] Industries which rely heavily on proprietary information also are more likely to enjoy considerable advantages from internalization.[7] Thus, banks generally possess considerable potential for internalization advantages.

Banks can achieve internalization advantages from multinationalization in five areas: availability and cost of fund transfers within the MNB, efficient customer contacts, transfer pricing manipulation, larger and improved networks of market information and commercial intelligence, and the potential for reduced earnings variability.[8] Many of the internalization advantages available to banks have been achieved in a national market before the bank becomes multinational. Examples are centralized control, coordinated account management over a variety of different segments of the financial markets, and transfer of commercial intelligence within the national markets. Becoming multinational merely extends these advantages to new markets. Potential savings may increase, but the essential difference lies in the breadth and scale of operations rather than in the techniques themselves.[9]

Worldwide networks allow MNBs to substitute intrabank fund transfers for some fund transfers done in the external markets. This may result in reduced transaction costs and risks and increased flexibility in asset and liability management. This also makes it easier to exploit favorable interest rate differentials through arbitrage and to shift funds globally to their most profitable use.

Banking is a service industry where extensive intermediary information inputs are needed. A number of services provided for multinational customers require "orientation contacts" that entail a physical presence near the source of relevant information.[10] Orientation contacts require speed of interaction and are associated with face-to-face contacts. Foreign banking offices of MNBs, especially those in important national banking markets, facilitate such orientation contacts. Modern telecommunication facilities may supersede foreign banking offices in this matter to some extent, but only at some cost and in a limited way.[11]

Centrally coordinated control and global networks enable MNBs to evade unfavorable official restrictions of both home and host countries. They can arbitrarily realize high profits in lower tax countries through transfer price manipulation. Wide variations of interest rates in international interbank markets across banks and over time offer sufficient opportunity to manipulate transfer prices of funds. Besides tax savings, MNBs can overcome restrictions on capital flows and profit repatriation. The wider a bank's networks, the larger its potential for such internalization advantages.

MNBs generally have better ability to develop an internal global communication and information network than purely domestic banks. This provides MNBs with better abilities to scan globally for business opportunities and risks as a result of the continuous exchange of information within the system. This kind of information exchange is seldom possible in the external markets or, if it is possible, only insufficiently and belatedly. The sheer number of separate sources of commercial intelligence can provide a more efficient network of information with consequently increased profit opportunities.[12]

Operations in different national markets could also lower variability in MNB earnings compared to purely domestic banks.[13] This would be largely due to the broader opportunities for international diversification and the less-than-perfect correlation among national financial markets.

The magnitude of a bank's internalization benefits depends on the nature of its banking activities and the level of ownership advantages necessary for their successful performance. Banking activities which rely heavily on proprietary information are apt to afford greater opportunity for benefit from internalization, as the markets for information are generally characterized by significant imperfections. For example, borrowing and lending have more potential for internalization benefits than does issuing letters of credit, as borrowing and lending are more information-oriented. Furthermore, benefits from internalizing a certain banking activity vary across banks. Those banks with higher levels of the ownership advantages necessary for the successful execution of a certain banking activity can reap greater benefits from internalizing it than can banks with lower levels of such ownership advantages.

Most internalization theorists fail to recognize such dynamic aspects of internalization benefits. They assume that "the business of internalizing externalities" necessarily brings benefits and that the magnitude of such benefits depends on the degree of externalities involved in a certain transaction. Such theorists seem to believe that the nature of a transaction (degree of externalities) determines the kinds of transaction to be internalized or externalized and that banks can acquire the same magnitude of benefit from internalizing a given level of certain transactions since the same kind of transaction entails the same degree of externalities in a given market. This is a static approach. The magnitude of the internalization benefit of a certain transaction is not necessarily the same across banks. The magnitude depends on the level of individual banks' ownership advantages necessary for performing that transaction, which are the objects of internalization.

The three advantages have various determinants within them. Some of the determinants are not evenly spread across countries, banks, and time. Furthermore, some determinants of ownership-specific advantages and internalization advantages are closely related to each other and frequently inseparable, especially when measured with empirical data, as only internalized ownership advantages are empirically observable and measurable. Table 4-1 shows major determinants of each advantage and proposed ways of measuring them.

Ownership-specific and internalization advantages are bank-specific, whereas location-specific advantages are country-specific. These advantages are not static: they may change over time.[14] This may help explain why banks from particular countries tend to have more extensive multinational involvement, why the degrees of multinational involvement among banks from the same countries differ, why certain host countries can attract more MNBs than other countries, and what are important sources of MNB advantages to which purely domestic banks do not have access. Only with an eclectic approach to industrial organization, location, and internalization can the dynamic and complex multinational phenomenon in the banking industry be explained satisfactorily.

## Determinants of Major Multinational Banking Activities

The eclectic model hypothesizes that the various advantages are not equally important for all banking activities of MNBs. Some advantages are more important for certain banking activities, while others are more relevant for other activities. Based on the concepts and the determinants of three strands of advantages developed in the eclectic model, one can identify the relations of the various advantages with the major MNB banking activities.

Major activities differ among MNBs, since their activities are formulated and conducted in such a way as to achieve a maximum use of resources under constrained situations. The three advantages of the eclectic model represent such resources and constraints (or opportunities), and as the three advantages are not evenly spread across banks, banking activities conducted by individual banks are not necessarily similar among themselves. Actually, banking activities tend to be different across banks and locations of operations. Taking this into consideration, relations between these advantages and some major multinational banking activities discussed in chapter 2—deposit taking, interbank funding, commercial and industrial lending, sovereign lending, project financing, foreign exchange trading, and management of syndicated

Table 4-1.   Major Determinants of Ownership, Location, and
Internalization Advantages of MNBS

A.   Ownership Advantages

1.   Size of a bank

a.   Size of a bank's capital or domestic deposits

2.   Access to funding sources of major currencies

a.   Size of major currency deposits.

3.   Knowledge and experience in multinational banking operations

a.   Size of bank's foreign lending and deposits

4.   Knowledge and experience of a particular market

a.   Number of years of banking operations in the particular
market

5.   Scope of a bank's international netowrk

a.   Number of foreign offices of a bank

b.   Number of countries in which a bank has offices

6.   A bank's creditworthiness

a.   Bank rankings

7.   Availability of skilled personnel

a.   Skilled (international banking officer)/Total employee
ratio

b.   Amount of syndicated lendings (or foreign exchange
trading)/Total lendings

8.   Product differentiability

a.   Expenditures on marketing & product
development/Operating income ratio

Table 4-1

9. Possession of customers with high international involvement

    a. Customer groups' foreign sales (or assets)/Customer groups' domestic sales (or assets)

B. Location Advantages

    1. Interest rate differentials (deposit & lending rates)

        a. Differences between home and host interest rates

    2. Tax rate differentials

        a. Differences between home and host tax rates.

    3. Expected changes in exchange rate

        a. $\Delta \dfrac{\text{host currency}}{\text{home currency (unit)}}$

    4. Size of host banking markets

        a. Host GNP or size of total deposits of host banking system

    5. Market competitiveness (home & host markets)

        a. Market concentration ratio

        b. Average interest spreads

    6. Size of host country foreign trade (exports and imports)

        a. Size of total foreign trade

        b. Size of trade with home country (or a bank's customers)

    7. Size of foreign direct investment

        a. Size of total FDI in host country

        b. Size of home country (or a bank customers') FDI in host country

Table 4-1 (continued)

8. Restrictiveness of banking regulations (home & host countries)

    a. Host banking regulations on foreign banks: restrictive or non-restrictive

    b. Home banking regulations on international operations of home banks: restrictive or non-restrictive

9. Similarity of business practices

    a. Similarity of banking system

    b. Similarity of communication methods (language)

10. Nationality of a bank

C. Internalization Advantages

1. Degree of control of foreign operations

    a. Ownership share

2. Economies of internal operations

    a. Amount of intra-bank transaction (borrowings & lendings)/total bank assets ratio

    b. Amount of assets and liabilities to directly related institutions of a foreign office

3. Availability and size of intra-bank funding facilities

    a. Funding stability at offshore banking markets - Number of offshore markets in which a bank has offices

    b. Amount of inter-bank borrowings/a bank's total assets

loans—are presented in table 4-2 within the context of the eclectic model. Only direct and primary relations are considered, though most advantages seem to be related to most banking activities in one way or another with different degrees of strength.

Certain advantages have extensive relations with various banking activities. Degree of control of foreign operations, access to funding sources of major currencies, knowledge of and experience in multinational banking, availability of skilled personnel, banking regulations of home and host countries, and availability of internal market seem to be related to major multinational banking activities more extensively than other advantages. Some banking activities tend to need services of a more extensive range of advantages than others. Commercial and industrial lending (both local and foreign currencies) and foreign exchange trading seem to require a wider range of advantages to be successfully performed. These activities allow MNBs with extensive advantages to exploit those advantages to the maximum extent. Nevertheless, almost all multinational activities seem to need services of a combination of some elements of the three advantages.

Some of these relationships, described in table 4-2, can be highlighted by simple comparisons among the fifteen largest U.S. banks (table 4-3). Although these relationships are not clearly identifiable among the top five largest banks, they are identifiable, to some extent, among the rest. The size of a bank's equity capital seems to be relatively less closely related to the level of a bank's syndicated loan management than such factors as the scope of a bank's international network and the availability and size of intrabank funding and information channels. For instance, Security Pacific Bank, which is the eighth largest bank in the U.S., is far behind Bankers Trust Co., which is the ninth largest, in the number of Eurocurrency syndicated loans managed during the period from 1975 to 1980. This seems primarily due to Bankers Trust's extensive international networks (and experience in multinational banking) and internal funding and information channels, along with its skilled personnel which are not shown in the table. Such patterns can also be found from the comparisons between Continental Illinois Bank and Bankers Trust Co. and between Irving Trust Co. and Mellon Bank. These comparisons also show the relationship between major advantages and overseas lending and deposit-taking activities. However, more rigorous investigation of such relationships will be done in the next chapter.

## An Eclectic Model of MNB Growth

An eclectic model hypothesizes that the growth (level of multinational involvement) of a multinational bank in a particular market is determined by a particular combination of the bank's ownership-specific, location-specific, and

Table 4-2. Types of Advantages for Major Multinational Banking Activities

| Types of Advantages | Major multinational banking activities | | | | | | | | |
|---|---|---|---|---|---|---|---|---|---|
| | Customer deposit taking (onshore) | Customer deposit taking (offshore) | Inter-bank funding | Commercial & Industrial lending (local currency) | Commercial & Industrial lending (foreign currency) | Sovereign lending | Project financing | Foreign exchange trading | Management of syndicated loans |
| **A. Ownership Advantages** | | | | | | | | | |
| 1. Size of a bank | X | | X | | | | | | |
| 2. Access to funding sources of major currencies | | | | | X | X | X | | |
| 3. Knowledge & experience of multinational banking | | | X | | X | X | X | X | X |
| 4. Knowledge & experience of a particular market | X | | | X | | | | | |
| 5. Scope of a bank's international network | | X | X | | | | | X | X |
| 6. A bank's creditworthiness | X | X | X | | | | | | X |
| 7. Availability of skilled personnel | | | X | | | X | X | X | X |
| 8. Product differentiability | | | | | | X | X | | |
| 9. Possession of customer groups with high int'l involvement | | | | | X | | | X | X |
| **B. Location Advantages** | | | | | | | | | |
| 1. Interest rate differentials | X | | | X | X | | | | |
| 2. Tax rate differentials | | | | X | X | | | | X |
| 3. Expected changes in exchange rate | | | | X | X | | | X | |

Table 4-2 (continued)

| | Customer deposit taking (onshore) | Customer deposit taking (offshore) | Inter-bank funding | Comm'l & Indust'l lending (local curr.) | Comm'l & Indust'l lending (foreign curr.) | Sovereign lending | Project financing | Foreign exchange trading | Management of syndicated loans |
|---|---|---|---|---|---|---|---|---|---|
| 4. Size of host banking market | X | | | X | X | | | | |
| 5. Market competitiveness (home) | | X | X | | X | | | | |
| 6. Market competitiveness (host) | X | | | X | X | | | | |
| 7. Size of host country foreign trade | | | | | X | | | X | |
| 8. Size of FDI in host country | | | | X | X | | | X | |
| 9. Restrictiveness of banking regulations (home) | X | X | X | | X | X | | | |
| 10. Restrictiveness of banking regulations (host) | X | | | X | X | | | | |
| 11. Similarity of business practices | X | | | X | X | | | | |
| 12. Nationality of a bank | X | X | | | | | | X | |
| C. Internalization Advantages | | | | | | | | | |
| 1. Degree of control of foreign operations | X | X | X | X | X | X | X | X | X |
| 2. Economies of internal operations | | | X | X | X | X | X | X | X |
| 3. Availability and size of intra-bank funding facilities | X | | | X | X | X | X | X | X |

Table 4-3. Comparison of the Levels of Multinational Banking Activities and Selected Advantages of 15 Largest U.S. Banks

| Banks | Major Banking Activities | | | Types of Advantages | | | |
| | # of eurocurrency syndicated loans lead- or co-managed from 1975 to 1980 | Loans at overseas offices (US$m.) | Deposits at overseas offices (US$m.) | Size of equity capital (US$m.) | Size of domestic deposits (US$m.) | # of countries in which a bank has branches | # of offshore markets in which a bank has offices |
|---|---|---|---|---|---|---|---|
| 1. Citibank | 433 (2) | 26,587(1) | 40,385(1) | 3,520(1) | 18,779(3) | 73.8(1) | 12(1) |
| 2. BCA | 360 (3) | 18,907(3) | 31,940(2) | 3,129(2) | 40,341(1) | 44.8(2) | 9(2) |
| 3. Chase Manhattan | 451 (1) | 19,017(2) | 23,815(3) | 2,311(3) | 21,655(2) | 34.5(3) | 8.7(3) |
| 4. Morgan Guaranty | 223 (5) | 9,602(5) | 14,098(4) | 1,624(4) | 12,638(7) | 11.5(7) | 6.7(6) |
| 5. Manufac. Hanover | 275 (4) | 10,504(4) | 12,982(5) | 1,416(5) | 18,648(4) | 11.8(6) | 6.3(7) |
| 6. Continental Ill. | 118 (10) | 5,154(8) | 9,055(7) | 1,185(6) | 11,069(9) | 10.8(8) | 4.7(12) |
| 7. Chemical | 219 (6) | 6,491(6) | 10,142(6) | 1,156(7) | 14,536(5) | 12.3(5) | 7.8(4) |
| 8. Security Pacific | 94 (11) | 2,418(10) | 3,235(13) | 1,059(8) | 12,964(6) | 5.8(12) | 4.8(11) |
| 9. Bankers Trust | 181 (7) | 5,586(7) | 8,879(8) | 997(9) | 10,186(10) | 7.5(9) | 7(5) |
| 10. FNB Chicago | 127 (9) | 4,887(9) | 7,378(9) | 960(10) | 8,601(11) | 17.2(4) | 6.2(8) |
| 11. Mellon Bank | 4 (15) | 891(15) | 2,385(14) | 680(11) | 6,189(14) | 4.5(13) | 3(14) |
| 12. Wells Fargo | 140 (8) | 2,069(12) | 1,779(15) | 675(12) | 11,746(8) | 3.7(15) | 4(13) |
| 13. Marine Midland | 37 (13) | 2,320(11) | 3,875(12) | 590(13) | 7,296(13) | 6.0(11) | 5.8(9) |
| 14. Crocker | 91 (12) | 1,496(14) | 4,602(10) | 582(14) | 8,074(12) | 4.2(14) | 3(14) |
| 15. Irving Trust | 18 (14) | 1,704(13) | 3,889(11) | 464(15) | 5,918(15) | 6.5(10) | 5(10) |

Note: 1. Relative rankings in parentheses.
2. All figures are averages from 1975 to 1980, unless specified otherwise.

Source: Individual bank's *Annual Reports and 10-K Reports.*
*Euromoney*, various issues.

internalization advantages that prevail at a given time and place. The general form of the hypothesis can be expressed as:

$$DV_{ijkt} = f\left(IVO_{fjt},\ IVL_{gjkt},\ IVI_{hjt}\right),$$

where

$DV_{ijkt} =$     Dependent variable $i$ (size or form of involvement) of a bank $j$ in a host market $k$ at time $t$.

$IVO_{fjt} =$     Ownership-specific advantage factor $f$ of a bank $j$ at time $t$.

$IVL_{gjkt} =$     Location-specific advantage factor $g$ of a bank $j$ in a host market $k$ at time $t$.

$IVI_{hjt} =$     Internalization advantage factor $h$ of a bank $j$ at time $t$.

A linear relationship is assumed, since there are no strong reasons to assume any other functional form.

An operational form of the eclectic model is developed below, with regard to the selection and measurement of major variables and their relationships with level of multinational involvement. The model will be used to identify empirically major determinants of U.S. MNBs in the next chapter.

*Level of Multinational Involvement: Dependent Variables*

The level of multinational involvement is represented by the size and performance of an MNBs's foreign branches. This is mainly because a foreign branch is a major organizational form of multinational involvement of MNBs, and the limited banking activities of representative offices and agencies and the widely diverse operations of foreign subsidiaries make it difficult to maintain consistency and comparability in testing the model empirically. Four different aspects of the size-and-performance-of-branch concepts constitute the dependent variables of the model: *the size of branch total assets* (DV$_1$), *the size of branch lending* (DV$_2$), *the size of branch deposits accepted* (DV$_3$), and *branch profitability* (DV$_4$). The reason four different aspects of branch operations are studied is to reflect the diverse strategic emphasis of individual MNBs in establishing branch offices in particular overseas markets. Four different patterns of MNB strategic emphasis regarding foreign branch activities are discernible: (1) to secure funding sources; (2) to establish lending outlets; (3) to create revenue generators; and (4) to achieve a combination of the above three. Size of branch total assets (DV$_1$) takes into account the fourth strategic emphasis, while size of branch lending (DV$_2$), size of branch deposits accepted (DV$_3$), and branch profitability (DV$_4$) consider largely the first, the second and the third emphases, respectively.

*Various Advantage Factors: Independent Variables*

The choice of independent variables is basically done on the basis of major determinants examined previously (table 4-1), but is heavily influenced by the availability of necessary data. The greatest difficulties in gathering necessary data on individual banks are that some important data are simply unavailable for confidentiality reasons and some available published data are too general for one to extract any useful meaning from them.

*Ownership-specific advantages.* The size of a bank's equity capital (IVO$_1$), the size of a bank's domestic deposits in a home country (IVO$_2$), the scope of a bank's multinational network (IVO$_3$), and its multinational banking experience and technology (IVO$_4$) are selected as determinants of ownership-specific advantages in this model.

*Size of a bank's equity capital (IVO$_1$).* A bank's equity capital is a basis for overall banking business; the size of it determines the magnitude of overall banking operations. This is measured by the share of a bank's equity capital in its home banking market and is expected to have a positive relationship with the level of a bank's multinational involvement. The reason is that as the scale of domestic banking increases, one might expect the scale of most aspects of banking to increase, including multinational business. Only if attracting foreign business is a substitute for attracting domestic business would one expect this relationship not to hold.

*Size of a bank's domestic deposits (IVO$_2$).* This is measured by the share of a bank's total domestic demand, time, and savings deposits in the home country. Size of domestic deposits is expected to have a positive coefficient unless domestic deposits substitute for foreign deposits, as the parent's domestic deposits in the home country act as one of the major funding sources for multinational lending and assets in foreign branches through the network of intrabank markets.

*Scope of a bank's multinational network (IVO$_3$).* The wider a bank's multinational network, the more opportunities the bank may have to expand its foreign branch operations, as it may have enhanced scanning ability to find worldwide business opportunities or to reduce business risks through global diversification. Therefore, scope of network is expected to have a positive relationship with the dependent variables. This variable is measured in terms of the number of countries in which a bank has branch offices.

*Multinational banking experience and technology (IVO$_4$).* Here, technology generally refers to a bank's ability to differentiate its products, managerial capability, trained personnel, and marketing ability. Though there are relatively fewer opportunities for a bank to differentiate its products compared with a manufacturing firm, superior managerial capability and marketing competency may give a bank an edge over its competitors in the market. This would be appropriately measured by either the proportion of international banking officers among a bank's staff or the share of a bank's expenditures on training, marketing, and product development to its total operating income. But the paucity of information on these factors forces an alternate means of measurement: the number of Eurocurrency syndicated loans lead-managed or comanaged by a bank. This is an acceptable proxy as the lead management of Eurocurrency syndicated loans requires a high degree of advanced banking technologies and experiences such as competent human resources, sophisticated money market and foreign exchange market operations, and extensive information on borrowers and participating banks. This variable is expected to influence the dependent variables positively.

*Location-specific advantages.* Location-specific advantages refer to the kinds of advantages which a bank can acquire from certain locations simply because it has relations with those locations at a specific time. These advantages are usually expressed in terms of differentials between two locations.

*Interest rate differentials (IVL$_1$).* Interest rate differentials between host and home countries are considered in two different areas: deposit rates and lending rates. The greater the deposit rate differentials between host and home countries, the greater the expected effort by a bank to obtain deposits in the home country, if other things are equal. However, the greater the lending rate differentials between host and home countries, the greater the expected effort by home banks to lend in overseas host markets. Consequently the deposit rate differentials (IVL$_1$-D: host deposit rates – home deposit rates) are expected to have a negative coefficient with regard to the relevant dependent variables, whereas the lending rate differentials (IVL$_1$-L: host lending rates – home lending rates) may have a positive coefficient.

The host deposit rates are approximated by the three-month certificate of deposit (CD) rate, or the three-month time deposit rate if the three-month CD rate is unavailable (in host offshore markets, Eurodollar 3-month CD rate), in host markets. The home (in this case, U.S.) deposit rates are proxied by the three-month CD rate. The CD rate is a better proxy for deposit rates in the U.S. money market than the Treasury bill (T-bill) rate in this case, because T-bills are issued by the U.S. government, which is hardly representative of U.S. issuing institutions in general. The host lending rates are measured in terms of the host prime rate. In the case of host offshore markets, the host lending rates are measured in terms of the Eurodollar prime loan rate, which usually is Eurodollar three-month CD rate plus 0.5 percentage point of margin.[15] The home lending rates are approximated by the effective U.S. prime rate which usually is 20 percent above the U.S. prime rate to cover the cost of maintaining compensatory balances.[16] These deposit and lending rate differentials can be expressed more clearly in the following way:

$IVL_1$-D:      Host 3-month CD rate (or 3-month time deposit rate) – U.S. 3-month CD rate. In the case of host offshore markets, Eurodollar 3-month CD rate is used.

$IVL_1$-L:      Host prime rate[17] – Effective U.S. prime rate ($1.2 \times$ U.S. prime rate). In the case of host offshore markets, Eurodollar prime loan rate (Eurodollar 3-month CD rate plus 0.5 percentage point).

*Expected exchange rate changes ($IVL_2$).* If the exchange rate, measured by the value of the U.S. dollar in host currencies, increases—that is, if host currencies depreciate vis-à-vis the U.S. dollar—the cost of taking deposits in host currencies abroad for U.S. banks decreases in dollar terms, other things being equal. Thus, an expectation of a higher exchange rate would lead to increased efforts to obtain host currency deposits and liabilities in host markets. It could imply a positive coefficient with regard to $DV_3$ (branch deposits accepted). However, since $DV_3$ may include deposits in nonhost currencies, the effect of the exchange rate variable may be partially obscured. The effects of this variable on other dependent variables are unclear because the net effects depend on the denominational composition of branch assets and liabilities. In offshore markets, this variable is not expected to be relevant, as the U.S. dollar is the predominant currency of transaction. This variable is proxied by the rate of changes in ex post exchange rates.

When the foreign exchange market and the domestic money market are closely integrated with each other in host countries, as is frequently the case in major developed countries, effective interest rate differentials would be more relevant than the separate use of this variable and interest rate differential variables ($IVL_1$). However, where the host foreign exchange market and domestic money market are relatively independent of each other, as they are in most developing countries adopting a controlled foreign exchange rate regime, these two variables should be used separately to identify their respective relationships with the level of a bank's multinational involvement.

*Size of host banking markets ($IVL_3$).* The size of host banking markets may act as a positive factor for the growth of foreign branch activities in the host banking markets. Large host banking markets surely will encourage foreign banks to expand into those markets. The size of host banking markets is measured in terms of the size of the GDP (gross domestic product) of the host country in the case of onshore banking and the aggregate GDP of the region in the case of offshore banking.

*Amount of foreign trade of host countries (IVL₄)*. As foreign trade-related financing is one of the most important international banking activities of commercial banks, the amount of host country foreign trade is expected to be positively related to the size of multinational banking activity. This variable is measured as the amount of host country exports to and imports from the U.S. However, as foreign trade financing is not an important business in offshore banking markets, this variable is not expected to be significant in the case of offshore markets.

*Amount of foreign direct investment in host countries (IVL₅)*. Greater FDI in host countries, especially from the home country, increases the potential of business for MNBs. Servicing multinational customers' overseas banking needs is generally regarded as one of major motivations of MNBs to go overseas. Therefore, this variable is expected to relate positively to the size of multinational banking activity. This variable is measured by the relative size of outstanding U.S. FDI in the host country. As with IVL₄, the outstanding U.S. FDI in the host country is used in the case of onshore banking and the aggregate U.S. FDI figures in the region are used in the case of offshore banking.

*Host country regulations on branch banking operations of foreign banks (IVL₆-M)*. This dummy variable represents the restrictiveness of host regulations on foreign banks in that country. It might be ideal to analyze the separate effects of specific regulations, but such analysis is beyond the scope of this study. If general regulatory environments of the host country are restrictive, this variable has a value of "1." If not, it has a value of "0." It is hypothesized that general regulatory environments would be restrictive in the case of onshore banking and not restrictive in the case of offshore banking. A positive coefficient is expected if the regulatory framework encourages branch operations of foreign banks; a negative one is expected if it discourages them.

*Degree of competition in banking markets (IVL₇)*. Highly oligopolistic banking markets tend to pose severe entry barriers to banks that want to enter the markets. But in offshore banking markets, entry barriers of this kind are expected to be negligible as free competition there is the name of the game. Conversely, highly oligopolistic banking environments tend to provide incentives to banks based in that market to go overseas.[18] The degree of competition is measured by market concentration ratios, which are estimated by the share of the five largest banks' assets in the market. A higher concentration ratio in the host banking market (IVL₇) is expected to have a negative effect on the growth of foreign banks' activities in the host onshore banking market. A higher concentration ratio in the home banking market may have an encouraging effect on the growth of multinational activities of home banks in foreign countries including the host country. But the latter is not used in the test as the study concerns banks from the same home country (U.S.). In a comparative study which explores different patterns of multinational involvement of banks from different countries, this factor would be an important explanatory variable.

Other than the above locational factors which are used in testing the eclectic model in this study, the following locational factors could also be considered in appropriate studies on MNBs: (1) tax rate differentials, (2) differences in business environments, such as banking system and regulatory frameworks, and (3) home country banking regulations. Higher tax rates in host countries may discourage multinational operations of banks there, other things being equal. However, in this study, since host countries either have tax treaties with the U.S. government or provide tax exemptions, impacts on branch activities of any tax rate differentials may not be significant as U.S. banks have to pay any tax differentials between host and home countries to the U.S. government when the branch incomes are repatriated to the U.S., if the tax paid in host countries is smaller than that under the U.S. tax system.

Foreign banks operating in host markets whose business environments are similar to those of home countries would be expected to have competitive advantages over banks from countries of totally dissimilar business environments. Home country banking regulations may or may not restrict foreign activities of home banks, which, in turn, give home banks competitive advantages or disadvantages vis-à-vis banks from other countries whose regulatory restrictiveness is different from that of home countries.

*Internalization advantages.* Economies of internal operations ($IVI_1$) and availability and size of intrabank funding facilities ($IVI_2$) are used as major determinants of internalization advantages. As this study concerns only branch banking operations, degree of control and share of equity involvement are not used as internalization advantages because all banks have the same degree of control over their branches (at least, nominally) and the same 100 percent equity involvement.

*Economies of internal operations ($IVI_1$).* Availability of internal markets, which generally incur lower transaction costs than external markets, gives an edge to the possessor banks over their competitors with limited or no internal markets. Thus, this variable is expected to have a positive coefficient. This variable is measured by the amount of assets due from and liabilities due to directly related institutions (the parent and other branches of the parent) of a foreign branch.

*Availability and size of intrabank funding facilities ($IVI_2$).* Well developed and wider internal factor (or intermediate product) markets enable a firm to achieve economies of internal markets as the firm can have a secure supply source at lower costs. This enables the firm to produce better and less costly products. Similarly, a bank with a well-developed and wider network in offshore banking markets may have more opportunities to obtain high quality loanable funds. The network in offshore banking markets helps the bank to gain access to information and business sources more easily, too. The number of offshore banking markets[19] in which a bank has offices is used as a proxy for the degree of internal transactions. As a bank may obtain additional advantages from the possession of such internal funding sources, this variable is expected to have a positive coefficient.

These are the independent variables to be used in the model. A summary list of these appears in table 4-4. Some variables are expressed in relative forms to avoid inflationary effects and foreign exchange translation effects.

However, some flexibility in the model as to the specific variables to be incorporated into it is needed, depending on the research questions it must address. Particularly, location advantage variables need some modification when this model is used to investigate some of the study questions. As it is extremely difficult to get information on location advantages of individual banks in the host markets, this study assumes that all U.S. banks face the same opportunities for all location advantages in a particular host market at a particular time, though banks actually face different opportunities in some location advantages. Different business involvement of a bank's home customers in the host market and different effective interest and tax rates actually create different opportunities for location advantages, even among banks of the same nationality, in a specific host market at a given time. This assumption may in some cases limit the applicability of the eclectic model as it is developed here, depending on research questions.

In the next chapter, empirical tests of the eclectic model with experiences of U.S. MNBs in two Asia Pacific countries (Singapore and Korea) will be conducted to answer the study questions raised earlier, and the results of these tests will be investigated and interpreted.

Table 4-4. List of Variables

| Variables | Proxies | Expected sign of coefficient |
|---|---|---|
| *Dependent Variables* | | |
| DV$_1$: Size of branch assets | Total branch assets/Total host commercial bank assets | |
| DV$_2$: Size of branch lendings | Total branch lendings/Total host commercial bank lendings | |
| DV$_3$: Size of branch deposits accepted | Total branch deposits/Total host commercial bank deposits | |
| DV$_4$: Size of branch net operating income | Branch operating income/Total branch assets | |
| *Independent Variables* | | |
| I. Ownership advantages | | |
| IVO$_1$: Size of a bank's equity capital | A bank's equity capital /Total U.S. commercial bank equity capital | + |
| IVO$_2$: Size of a bank's domestic deposits | A bank's domestic deposits /Total U.S. commercial bank domestic deposits | + |
| IVO$_3$: Size of a bank's multinational network | Number of countries in which a bank has branch offices | + |
| IVO$_4$: Multinational banking experience and technology | Number of Eurocurrency syndicated loans lead managed or comanaged by the bank since 1973 | + |
| II. Location advantages | | |
| IVL$_1$: Interest rate differentials between host & home countries | | |
| IVL$_1$D: Deposit rate differentials | Host 3-month CD rate (or 3-month time deposit rate) – U.S. 3-month CD rate. In case of offshore banking, Eurodollar 3-month CD rate. | – |
| IVL$_1$L: Lending rate differentials between host and home countries | Host prime rate – Effective U.S. prime rate (1.2 × U.S. prime rate). In case of offshore banking, Eurodollar prime rate (Eurodollar 3-month CD rate plus 1/2 percentage point). | + |

Table 4-4. (continued)

| Variables | Proxies | Expected sign of coefficient |
|---|---|---|
| IVL$_2$: Expected exchange rate changes | $$\frac{\text{Exchange rate}_t - \text{Exchange rate}_{t-1}}{\text{Exchange rate}_{t-1}}$$ where exchange rate is expressed as a unit value of the U.S. dollar in host currencies | $+$ or indeterminate |
| IVL$_3$: Relative size of host banking markets | Host GDP/U.S. GDP (constant price). In case of offshore banking, GDP of the region instead of host GDP. | $+$ |
| IVL$_4$: Size of foreign trade of host countries | Host exports and imports / Host GDP with U.S. (current price) | $+$ |
| IVL$_5$: Size of FDI in host countries | U.S. FDI in the / Host GDP (current price) host country | $+$ |
| IVL$_6$-M: Host country regulations on branch banking operations of foreign banks | Dummy variable: "1" if restrictive "0" if not | $+$ or $-$ |
| IVL$_7$: Host banking market concentration ratio | Share of 5 largest banks' assets | $-$ |
| III. Internalization advantages | | |
| IVI$_1$: Economies of internal operations | Amount of assets and liabilities/Total branch assets to directly related institutions (U.S. parent & other branches) | $+$ |
| IVI$_2$: Availability and size of of intrabank funding facilities | Number of offshore banking markets in which a bank has offices | $+$ |

# 5

# Empirical Tests of the Eclectic Model

## Data Sources and Methods

The sample consists of all U.S. banks which had branch banking operations in two Asia Pacific countries (Singapore and Korea) and reported to the Federal Reserve Board. Excluded from the sample is the American Express Corporation (AMEX) which had branches in the two countries, but whose domestic operations do not qualify AMEX as a U.S. commercial bank for reporting purposes.

Data for the dependent variables were obtained from financial statements of U.S. bank branches in host countries, which branches in Korea filed at the Bank of Korea and branches in Singapore filed at SGV & Co. of Manila, Philippines. Data on ownership advantages ($IVO_1$, $IVO_2$, $IVO_3$) and internalization advantages ($IVI_2$) were obtained from the banks' annual reports and 10-K reports, *Moody's Bank & Finance Manual, Polk's World Bank Directory*, the *Federal Reserve Bulletin*, and individual banks. Average figures would be more desirable for the purpose of the test, but they are usually not disclosed on a bank level. Average figures are available only on a banking corporation level, and hence usually include various nonbanking activities. Information on bank performance in managing Eurocurrency syndicated loans ($IVO_4$) was obtained from *Euromoney*, which regularly publishes statistics on major manager banks of Eurocurrency syndicated loans.

Interest rate information ($IVL_1$-D, $IVL_1$-L) was obtained from Morgan Guaranty's *World Financial Markets* and the host country's statistics (*Quarterly Bulletin* of the Monetary Authority of Singapore, *Monthly Statistical Bulletin* of the Bank of Korea). Information on foreign exchange rates and GDP came from *International Financial Statistics* of the International Monetary Fund (IMF). Trade data were found in the IMF's *Direction of Trade Statistics*. Data on U.S. foreign direct investment in the host countries and the Asia Pacific region were obtained from *Selected Data on the U.S. Direct Investment Abroad*, 1970-76 (Bureau of Economic Analysis, U.S. Dept. of Commerce, May 1982), *Survey of Current Business*, August 1981 and supplement titled *Revised Data Series on U.S. Direct Investment Abroad,* 1966-78 of the U.S. Department of Commerce, *Economic Yearbook of the Republic of China* (Economic Daily News of Taipei) and *Korean Economic Yearbook 1979 & 1981* (The Federation of Korean Industries of Seoul).

Finally, information on the advantages of economies of internal operations (IVI$_1$) was collected from financial statements of U.S. bank branches in the host countries filed at host central banking systems and SGV & Co. of Manila. However, the data collected are subject to several limitations. First, most financial data cannot be compared completely due to different accounting practices between periods, individual banks, and countries of operation. Second, the necessity of consulting different sources for the same series of data hurts the consistency and comparability of these data. Third, using year-end figures incurs the risk that the data may reflect seasonal effects. These weaknesses are partly corrected by the use of relative terms. However, such limitations are inevitable in this type of research, and would not be expected to affect the research results in a serious way.

Two sets of statistical tests (multiple regression) were conducted: (1) cross-nation and bank level (cross-section tests) and (2) cross-bank level (pooled time series cross-section tests). Due to the assumption of common location-specific advantages for all U.S. banks' branches in each host country at a given time, the effects of individual location-specific advantage factors could not be examined by the cross-section tests alone (problems of "singular matrix"). Thus, pooled time series cross-section tests in each host country were added. Three separate annual (1975, 1978, 1980) data sets were selected to stabilize the test results over time and for their significance in both sets of statistical tests except the pooled tests on Korea. In the latter, eight annual (1973 through 1980) data sets were used to obtain a meaningful sample size. Before 1975, three major banks (Bank of America, Citibank, and Chase Manhattan Bank) had been overwhelmingly predominant in the region. The first significant expansion occurred in 1975 after the lift of U.S. restrictions on capital flows in early 1974. The second expansion came in 1978 when host countries began to relax their restrictive positions on foreign bank entry.

In addition, a mail survey was conducted among U.S. MNB branches in Singapore, Hong Kong, Taiwan, and Korea with regard to their major banking activities and their major sources of economic rents to confirm the findings of the statistical tests.

**Statistical Tests**

A set of tests was conducted to find major determinants of MNB growth. U.S. MNBs with branches in Singapore and Korea in 1975, 1978, and 1980 were selected as samples and a cross-section multiple regression analysis was done among them at the three time periods. As discussed before, individual location advantage variables could not be used in the test, as the assumption of common location advantages across banks in a particular market would cause computational problems. Instead, a net location advantage variable (IVLM) was incorporated as a dummy variable to find out the effects of general location advantages (or disadvantages) of each host market.

The data collected showed that some groups of variables revealed a high correlation among themselves (appendices A and B). In particular, $IVO_1$ (size of a bank's equity capital) was found to be highly significantly correlated with other ownership advantages ($IVO_2$, $IVO_3$, and $IVO_4$) and with $IVI_2$ (the availability and size of intrabank funding facilities). This seems to be due to the fact that a bank's equity capital is the basis of all banking operations,[1] and often only "internalized" ownership advantages are reflected in ex post bank performance data. Thus, some variables were selected over others for inclusion in the test. The selection was done mainly under the considerations of a variable's relation with both the dependent and other independent variables, its partial correlation with other variables, and its theoretical importance vis-à-vis other variables.[2] Consequently, $IVO_1$ (size of a bank's equity capital) and $IVI_1$ (economies of internal operations) were selected respectively as the best estimators of the level of a bank's ownership advantages and internalization advantages among the various ownership and internalization advantages explained in chapter 4. The results of this cross-section analysis are shown in table 5-1.

As a supplement to the cross-section analysis, a pooled time series cross-section analysis was also conducted to find out possible effects of individual location advantages among U.S. MNB branches in each host country (Singapore: 1975, 1978, and 1980; Korea: 1973 to 1980). This method seems to be one of a few ways to investigate the effects of individual location advantages under the current condition of the availability of necessary data. The use of data in relative terms helps to reduce the effects of serial trends, which frequently make the results of such a method difficult to interpret. Among the various location advantages discussed before, the data showed that $IVL_3$ (size of host banking markets), $IVL_4$ (amount of foreign trade of host countries with the U.S.), and $IVL_5$ (amount of home FDI in host countries) were highly correlated among themselves (appendix B). Consequently, only $IVL_3$ was included in the test. The regression results are shown in table 5-2.

In the cross-section test (table 5-1), $IVO_1$ (size of a bank's equity capital) and IVLM (net location advantages) are signficantly related to the three dependent variables ($IVO_1$ is statistically significant with regard to $DV_1$, $DV_2$, and $DV_3$ at the 1 percent level in all three periods and IVLM is statistically significant with regard to the four dependent variables at the 1 percent to 2.5 percent level), while $IVI_1$ (economies of internal operations) is significant with

Table 5-1.   Results: Cross-Section (Cross-Nation and Bank Level) Test

1975

$$DV_1 = -0.78 + 1.85 \ IVO_1 + 0.02 \ IVI_1 - 5.29 \ IVLM$$
$$\phantom{DV_1 =} [-1.24] \ [4.96]**** \ [1.32] \ [-4.65]****$$

$$F**** = 12.90, \ \bar{R}^2 = 0.68, \ N = 18$$

$$DV_2 = 0.56 + 0.79 \ IVO_1 + 0.01 \ IVI_1 - 1.81 \ IVLM$$
$$\phantom{DV_2 =} [1.27] \ [3.03]**** \ [0.67] \ [-2.27]***$$

$$F*** = 4.40, \ \bar{R}^2 = 0.37, \ N = 18$$

$$DV_3 = -1.04 + 2.37 \ IVO_1 + 0.02 \ IVI_1 - 7.45 \ IVLM$$
$$\phantom{DV_3 =} [-1.43]*[5.47]**** \ [0.92] \ [-5.63]****$$

$$F**** = 15.51, \ \bar{R}^2 = 0.72, \ N = 18$$

$$DV_4 = 0.22 + 0.13 \ IVO_1 - 0.01 \ IVI_1 + 0.43 \ IVLM$$
$$\phantom{DV_4 =} [1.82]** \ [1.81]** \ [-1.12] \ [1.93]**$$

$$F*** = 4.39, \ \bar{R}^2 = 0.37, \ N = 18$$

1978

$$DV_1 = -0.03 + 1.26 \ IVO_1 + 0.001 \ IVI_1 - 2.22 \ IVLM$$
$$\phantom{DV_1 =} [-0.1] \ [6.60]**** \ [0.14] \ [-3.10]****$$

$$F**** = 19.99, \ \bar{R}^2 = 0.73, \ N = 22$$

$$DV_2 = 0.39 + 0.58 \ IVO_1 + 0.01 \ IVI_1 - 1.42 \ IVLM$$
$$\phantom{DV_2 =} [1.47]* \ [3.84]****[0.96] \ [-2.52]***$$

$$F**** = 8.49, \ \bar{R}^2 = 0.52, \ N = 22$$

$$DV_3 = 0.40 + 1.19 \ IVO_1 - 0.004 \ IVI_1 - 2.86 \ IVLM$$
$$\phantom{DV_3 =} [0.69] \ [3.64]**** \ [-0.22] \ [-2.32]***$$

$$F**** = 7.23, \ \bar{R}^2 = 0.47, \ N = 22$$

$DV_4$     $-0.29 + 0.58\ IVO_1 - 0.006\ IVI_1 + 1.84\ IVLM$
          $[-0.43]\ [1.49]^*\qquad [-0.26]\qquad\quad [1.27]$

$F^* = 2.91,\ \bar{R}^2 = 0.21,\ N = 22$

1980

$DV_1 = 0.06 + 0.82\ IVO_1 + 0.007\ IVI_1 - 1.53\ IVLM$
      $[0.36]\ [10.53]^{****}\ [1.48]^*\qquad [-4.00]^{****}$

$F^{****} = 39.92,\ \bar{R}^2 = 0.81,\ N = 29$

$DV_2 = 0.01 + 0.56\ IVO_1 + 0.01\ IVI_1 - 1.63\ IVLM$
      $[0.04]\ [5.23]^{****}\quad [2.30]^{***}\ [-3.11]^{****}$

$F^{****} = 11.30,\ \bar{R}^2 = 0.53,\ N = 29$

$DV_3 = 0.09 + 0.71\ IVO_1 + 0.01\ IVI_1 - 2.33\ IVLM$
      $[0.34]\ [5.33]^{****}\quad [1.24]\qquad [-3.53]^{****}$

$F^{****} = 14.26,\ \bar{R}^2 = 0.59,\ N = 29$

$DV_4 = 0.02 + 0.13\ IVO_1 + 0.003\ IVI_1 + 1.25\ IVLM$
      $[0.12]\ [1.34]^*\qquad [0.63]\qquad\quad [2.60]^{****}$

$F^{****} = 19.84,\ \bar{R}^2 = 0.67,\ N = 29$


t - statistics in brackets

    * indicates significant at 10 per cent level.
   ** indicates significant at 5 per cent level.
  *** indicates significant at 2.5 per cent level.
 **** indicates significant at 1 per cent level.

Table 5-2. Results: Pooled Time Series Cross-Section (Cross–Bank Level) Test

Korea (1973-1980)

$$DV_1 = -1.3 + 0.48 \ IVO_1 - 0.001 \ IVI_1 - 0.04 \ IVL_1 D$$
$$[-0.36] \quad [9.67]**** \quad [-0.64] \qquad [-0.88]$$

$$+0.11 \ IVL_1 L + 0.01 \ IVL_2 + 0.82 \ IVL_3 - 0.01 \ IVL_7$$
$$[1.85]**' \qquad [2.14]*** \qquad [1.76]** \qquad [-0.13]$$

$$F**** = 24.82, \ \bar{R}^2 = 0.75, \ N = 39$$

$$DV_2 = -0.17 + 0.65 \ IVO_1 - 0.001 \ IVI_1 + 0.004 \ IVL_1 D$$
$$[-0.03] \quad [9.96]**** \quad [-0.64] \qquad [0.07]$$

$$+0.13 \ IVL_1 L + 0.01 \ IVL_2 + 0.19 \ IVL_3 - 0.01 \ IVL_7$$
$$[1.65]* \qquad [0.66] \qquad [0.32] \qquad [-0.23]$$

$$F**** = 37.43, \ \ \bar{R}^2 = 0.81, \ \ N = 39$$

$$DV_3 = \ 0.18 + 0.05 \ IVO_1 - 0.00 \ IVI_1 - 0.003 \ IVL_1 D$$
$$[0.25] \quad [5.35]**** \quad [-0.53] \qquad [-0.35]$$

$$+0.02 \ IVL_1 L + 0.002 \ IVL_2 + 0.16 \ IVL_3 - 0.01 \ IVL_7$$
$$[1.33]* \qquad [1.65]* \qquad [1.69]* \qquad [-0.65]$$

$$F**** = 9.56, \ \ \bar{R}^2 = 0.50, \ N = 39$$

$$DV_4 = -12.78 + 0.72 \ IVO_1 - 0.19 \ IVI_1 - 0.19 \ IVL_1 D$$
$$[-0.70] \quad [2.87]**** \quad [-0.83] \qquad [-0.83]$$

$$+0.002 \ IVL_1 L + 0.05 \ IVL_2 + 1.92 \ IVL_3 + 0.12 \ IVL_7$$
$$[0.01] \qquad [1.24] \qquad [0.83] \qquad [0.51]$$

$$F** = 2.64, \ \ \bar{R}^2 = 0.12, \ N = 39$$

Singapore (1975, 1978, 1980)

$$DV_1 = 4.20 + 1.39 \ IVO_1 + 0.01 \ IVI_1 - 1.12 \ IVL_1D$$
$$[0.02] \ [9.36]**** \quad [1.76]** \quad [-0.00]$$

$$- \ 0.09 \ IVL_1L - 0.48 \ IVL_3$$
$$[0.00] \quad\quad [-0.01]$$

$$F**** = 25.17, \quad \bar{R}^2 = 0.70, \quad N = 52$$

$$DV_2 = 4.29 + 0.57 \ IVO_1 + 1.35 \ IVI_1 - 1.05 \ IVL_1D$$
$$[0.02] \ [5.05]**** \quad [2.31]*** \quad [-0.00]$$

$$- \ 0.07 \ IVL_1L - 0.40 \ IVL_3$$
$$[0.00] \quad\quad [-0.01]$$

$$F**** = 18.27, \quad \bar{R}^2 = 0.49, \quad N = 52$$

$$DV_3 = 5.78 + 1.61 \ IVO_1 + 0.01 \ IVI_1 - 0.87 \ IVL_1D$$
$$[0.02] \ [7.91]**** \quad [0.92] \quad\quad [-0.00]$$

$$+ \ 0.11 \ IVL_1L - 0.64 \ IVL_3$$
$$[0.00] \quad\quad [-0.01]$$

$$F**** = 17.47, \quad \bar{R}^2 = 0.62, \quad N = 52$$

$$DV_4 = 0.54 + 0.03 \ IVO_1 + 0.00 \ IVI_1 - 0.12 \ IVL_1D$$
$$[0.01] \ [0.75] \quad\quad [0.06] \quad\quad [0.00]$$

$$- \ 0.005 \ IVL_1L - 0.03 \ IVL_3$$
$$[0.00] \quad\quad [-0.002]$$

$$F = 0.26, \quad \bar{R}^2 = 0.03, \quad N = 52$$

t - statistics in brackets

* indicates significant at 10 per cent level.
** indicates significant at 5 per cent level.
*** indicates significant at 2.5 per cent level.
**** indicates significant at 1 per cent level.

regard to $DV_2$ at the 2.5 percent level in 1980. Size of a bank's equity capital, $IVO_1$ shows a positive coefficient with regard to all the dependent variables in all tests, as expected. Economies of internal operations, $IVI_1$, shows as expected a positive coefficient with regard to the three dependent variables ($DV_1$, $DV_2$, and $DV_3$) at all times, with the statistically insignificant exception of $DV_3$ in 1978. $IVI_1$ does not show the expected positive sign with regard to $DV_4$ (branch profitability), but the coefficients are not statistically significant. IVLM shows a mixed response—negative with regard to $DV_1$, $DV_2$, and $DV_3$, and positive with regard to $DV_4$ in all tests. In the pooled time series cross-section test, $IVO_1$ shows the expected positive sign at all times. $IVI_1$ shows a mixed response, but mostly statistically insignificant. $IVL_1L$ shows the expected positive sign in the case of Korea, but a mixed response in the case of Singapore. Other individual location variables show a mixed but statistically insignificant response in all tests.

The size of a bank ($IVO_1$) is generally found to relate significantly and positively to the level of MNB involvement in host markets. Larger MNBs, which tend to have more extensive funding resources, wider multinational branch networks, and more multinational banking experience and technology, are more likely to have larger assets, lending, and deposits in their foreign branches. However, it seems that the size of a bank is not strongly related to the profitability of its foreign branches ($DV_4$). But any judgment on the relation should be made cautiously, since profitability of foreign branches tends to be affected by a bank's global strategies. Branch profitability can be artificially manipulated to realize optimal profit results for the bank as a whole. The importance of bank size in multinational banking is consistent with the finding of a previous study on the role of firm size in industrial firms' decision to invest abroad (Horst, 1972).

The scope of economies of internal operations ($IVI_1$) is not found to be significantly related to the level of MNB involvement in host markets, though the signs of coefficients show expected positive relations with regard to dependent variables except profitability ($DV_4$) in all test periods. One possible explanation for this may be that any existing internalization advantage effects might have been subsumed under the effects of ownership-specific advantages as quite frequently only "internalized" ownership-specific advantages are reflected in ex post bank performance data.

Net location advantages of host banking markets (IVLM) are found to act as a disadvantage with respect to the performance of MNB foreign branches, except with respect to their profitability. This may be due to the fact that banking is basically a regulated industry and the multinational sector tends to be more regulated than other sectors in the host banking markets. This finding implies that, despite the general efforts of both Singapore and Korea to provide MNBs with more favorable environments, there still seem to exist locational (including regulatory) barriers to their full growth. However, net locational effects are found to be favorable for foreign branches' profitability (DV$_4$). This can be interpreted to mean that though restrictive, the banking environments of the two host countries are relatively favorable for the profitability of MNB branches. This may be due to the host environments' contribution to the realization of profits in the two countries, or it may be that their relatively favorable environments—particularly low tax rates and negligible restrictions on profit repatriation—may have induced MNBs to realize a substantial share of their global profits in the books of their branches in the two countries. This also implies that host governments, especially in onshore banking markets, are more concerned with foreign dominance of local banking markets than with the earnings of foreign banks. The finding coincides with the general direction of host government policy in dealing with foreign banks, which centers on preserving independence of monetary policies within their countries.

In the pooled time series cross-section test (table 5-2), size of a bank (IVO$_1$) is again found to be significantly positively related to dependent variables other than profitability (DV$_4$). The scope of economies of internal operations (IVI$_1$) is generally not found to be significant, with positive and negative coefficients in each host market.

The effects of location advantage factors are found to be different among banking activities and between onshore (Korea) and offshore (Singapore) markets. In the onshore banking market the lending rate differential (IVL$_1$L), foreign exchange rate changes (IVL$_2$), and the size of the host banking market (IVL$_3$) are significantly positively related to the growth of assets of U.S. MNB branches. The lending rate differential is found to be significantly positively related to the growth of U.S. MNB branch lending, and exchange rate changes and the size of the host banking market are important for the growth of MNB deposits accepted in the host market. Higher local lending rates are instrumental to the growth of U.S. MNB branch lending and assets in the host onshore market. That the deposit rate differential is not significantly related to the growth of branch deposits appears to be due to the nature of deposits in the onshore banking market. They are mostly loan-related compensatory accounts and transitory deposits, which are relatively insensitive to deposit rate changes.

In the offshore banking market, no individual location advantage factors are found to be significantly related to the growth of U.S. MNB branches. This implies that, in general, the Singapore market has not provided U.S. MNBs with any significantly favorable location advantage relative to the U.S. market. This finding coincides with the result of Goldberg and Saunders's 1980 study which found that the offshore banking market (London) did not provide U.S. banks with any significant location advantages in the seventies. Any advantages emanating from minimal regulatory environments in the offshore market seem to have been offset by the narrower spreads in the market. Interest rate differentials (deposit and lending) are found to be insignificant factors relative to branch growth. This coincides with the belief that no significant effective interest differences exist between the Asian dollar market and the U.S. financial market. The test does not produce any meaningful results with regard to the profitability of MNB branches in both markets. The possibility of arbitrary realization (or removal) of profits in ( or from) the books of MNB branches in each market during the test periods may be one explanation for the poor results of the model.

## Major Sources of Economic Rents of MNBs

A survey was conducted among U.S. MNB branches in Singapore, Hong Kong, Taiwan, and Korea to find out their major banking activities and major sources of economic rents for these activities to confirm the findings of the statistical tests in the previous section. Questionnaires were mailed to managers of 51 U.S. MNB branches which operated in the four countries in 1980. The managers were asked to indicate important sources of economic rents for major banking activities at their branches. The list of sources of economic rents and banking activities discussed in table 4-2 was included in the questionnaire mailed. Twenty-two branches (eight in Singapore, five in Hong Kong, four in Taiwan, and five in Korea) responded to the mail questionnaires for a 43 percent return rate.

Although it is difficult to draw any concrete interpretations from the results of such an impressionistic survey, several interesting facts were found which can complement or highlight the findings of the statistical tests. The results are shown in tables 5-3, 5-4, and 5-5. The numbers shown in the matrix tables indicate the frequency with which a source is indicated as important for a specific banking activity. Total frequency on the right side of the tables indicates the number of times a source is pointed out as important for major banking activities of U.S. MNB branches in host markets. This implies the relative importance of the individual sources of economic rents in multinational banking. Total frequency at the bottom of the tables indicates the number of times a specific banking activity is designated as important for MNBs in host markets, implying the relative importance of individual banking activities in their branches.

Overall, several banking activities and sources of economic rents are listed as more important than others. Foreign currency wholesale lending, syndicated lending, foreign exchange trading and offshore deposit taking are listed as major banking activities. Availability of trained personnel, availability and extensiveness of internal transactions and information exchange, experiences in and knowledge of multinational banking, a bank's U.S. dollar deposit base at home, and effective interest rate differentials are indicated as important sources of economic rents for their multinational banking operations (table 5-3).

Major banking activities and major sources of economic rents for multinational banking operations are found to vary in different market conditions. In offshore markets (Singapore and Hong Kong), foreign currency wholesale lending, syndicated lending, and offshore deposit taking are listed as major banking activities, and availability of trained personnel, availability and extensiveness of internal markets for information and funds, and experiences in multinational banking are selected as important factors for multinational banking (table 5-4). In onshore markets (Taiwan and Korea), foreign currency wholesale lending, foreign exchange trading and local currency wholesale lending are regarded as the major banking activities; availability of trained personnel, size of the home country direct investment in the host country, availability and extensiveness of internal markets for information and funds, size of the host banking markets, and a bank's U.S. dollar deposit base at home are found to be important sources of economic rents in multinational banking (table 5-5).

These findings seem to provide a useful supplementary explanation for the findings of the statistical tests. The findings also confirm the hypothesis of the relationship between various advantages of the eclectic model and major banking activities of MNBs developed in table 4-2. Among various location advantages, effective interest rate differentials, size of home country FDI in host countries, and size of the host banking markets are listed as important sources of economic rents for multinational banking activities. This confirms several previous studies on causes of MNB growth.[3] Size of domestic U.S. dollar deposit base, experience in and knowledge of multinational banking, and availablity of trained personnel—found to be highly correlated with the size of a bank's capital in the statistical tests—are regarded as important ownership advantages in the survey. Availability and ease of intrabank transactions ($IVI_1$ in the statistical tests) and availability and extensiveness of internal information control system ($IVO_3$ and $IVI_2$, highly correlated with the size of a bank), are listed as important internalization advantages for major multinational banking activities.

In summary, the findings of the statistical tests and the survey generally support the hypotheses of the eclectic model on the determinants of MNB growth. Thus, it can be concluded that MNB growth is an outcome of the particular combination of ownership, location, and internalization advantages. Different growth patterns across MNBs, banking markets, and time are due to the fact that these advantages are dynamic and are not spread evenly across MNBs, banking markets, and time.

Table 5-3.  Major Sources of Economic Rents for Multinational Banking Activities (Offshore and Onshore)

| Source of economic rents | Deposit taking (onshore) | Deposit taking (offshore) | Wholesale lending (local currency) | Wholesale lending (foreign currencies) | Syndicated lending | Project financing | Consumer lending | Foreign exchange trading | Total frequency |
|---|---|---|---|---|---|---|---|---|---|
| | | | Primary banking activity | | | | | | |
| 1. Size of a bank's total capital | 1 | 10 | 2 | 7 | 7 | 1 | | | 28 |
| 2. Domestic (U.S.A.) U.S. dollar deposit base | | | 9 | 20 | 13 | 8 | | | 50 |
| 3. Experiences & knowledge of multinational banking | | 8 | 1 | 7 | 14 | 8 | | 7 | 45 |
| 4. Years of operations in the host markets | 10 | 6 | 10 | 4 | | | 1 | | 31 |
| 5. Breadth of multinational branch network | 1 | 1 | | 6 | 7 | 3 | | 3 | 21 |
| 6. Availability of trained personnel (int'l officers) | 1 | 6 | 1 | 15 | 18 | 12 | | 22 | 75 |
| 7. Effective interest rates differentials between host and home countries | 3 | 11 | 10 | 14 | 2 | | 1 | 1 | 42 |
| 8. Effective tax rates differentials between host and home countries | | 3 | 2 | 3 | 2 | 1 | | | 11 |
| 9. Size of the host country trade with the home country | 1 | | | 9 | | | | 1 | 11 |

Table 5-3 (continued)

| | Deposit taking (onshore) | Deposit taking (offshore) | Wholesale lending (local currency) | Wholesale lending (foreign currencies) | Syndicated lending | Project financing | Consumer lending | Foreign exchange trading | Total frequency |
|---|---|---|---|---|---|---|---|---|---|
| 10. Size of the home country direct investment in the host country | 7 | 1 | 11 | 12 | | | | | 31 |
| 11. Size of the host country total foreign trade | 1 | | 4 | 12 | 4 | | | 8 | 29 |
| 12. Size and depth of the host banking market | 5 | 3 | 6 | 11 | 7 | 2 | | 2 | 36 |
| 13. Host country banking regulations | | 9 | 1 | 5 | 1 | | | | 16 |
| 14. Nationality of a bank | 2 | 12 | | | 6 | | | 6 | 26 |
| 15. Availability and ease of intra-bank transactions | | | 3 | 19 | 16 | 6 | | 11 | 55 |
| 16. Breadth of offshore network | | 2 | | 11 | 12 | 2 | | 3 | 30 |
| 17. Availability and extensiveness of internal information control system | | 1 | | 11 | 16 | 8 | | 21 | 57 |
| Total Frequency | 32 | 73 | 60 | 166 | 135 | 51 | 2 | 85 | |

Note: Number indicates the degree of frequency a specific source is indicated as important for a specific banking activity.

Table 5-4.  Major Sources of Economic Rents for Multinational Banking Activities (Offshore)

| Source of economic rents | Deposit taking (onshore) | Deposit taking (offshore) | Wholesale lending (local currency) | Wholesale lending (foreign currencies) | Syndicated lending | Project financing | Consumer lending | Foreign exchange trading | Total frequency |
|---|---|---|---|---|---|---|---|---|---|
| 1. Size of a bank's total capital | 1 | 10 | | 4 | 6 | 1 | | | 22 |
| 2. Domestic(U.S.A.) U.S. dollar deposit base | | | 2 | 12 | 10 | 8 | | | 32 |
| 3. Experiences & knowledge of multinational banking | | 8 | 1 | 7 | 11 | 6 | | 4 | 37 |
| 4. Years of operations in the host markets | 5 | 6 | 5 | 1 | | | 1 | | 18 |
| 5. Breadth of multinational branch network | 1 | 5 | | 6 | 7 | 3 | | 2 | 20 |
| 6. Availability of trained personnel(int'l officers) | 1 | 6 | 1 | 12 | 12 | 9 | | 13 | 54 |
| 7. Effective interest rates differentials between host and home countries | 3 | 11 | 3 | 8 | 2 | | 1 | | 28 |
| 8. Effective tax rates differentials between host and home countries | | 3 | 2 | 3 | 2 | 1 | | | 11 |
| 9. Size of the host country trade with the home country | | | | 2 | | | | | 2 |

Table 5-4 (continued)

| | Deposit taking (onshore) | Deposit taking (offshore) | Wholesale lending (local currency) | Wholesale lending (foreign currencies) | Syndicated lending | Project financing | Consumer lending | Foreign exchange trading | Total frequency |
|---|---|---|---|---|---|---|---|---|---|
| 10. Size of the home country direct investment in the host country | 2 | 1 | 3 | 6 | | | | | 12 |
| 11. Size of the host country total foreign trade | 1 | | 2 | 5 | 3 | | | 3 | 14 |
| 12. Size and depth of the host banking market | 3 | 3 | 2 | 7 | 5 | 1 | | 1 | 22 |
| 13. Host country banking regulations | | 9 | | 4 | 1 | | | | 14 |
| 14. Nationality of a bank | 2 | 12 | | | 5 | | | 4 | 23 |
| 15. Availability and ease of intra-bank transactions | | | 2 | 12 | 13 | 5 | | 7 | 39 |
| 16. Breadth of offshore network | | 2 | | 8 | 10 | 2 | | 3 | 25 |
| 17. Availability and extensiveness of internal information control system | | 1 | | 11 | 12 | 7 | | 13 | 44 |
| Total Frequency | 19 | 73 | 23 | 108 | 99 | 43 | 2 | 50 | |

Note: Number indicates the degree of frequency a specific source is indicated as important for a specific banking activity.

Table 5-5.   Major Sources of Economic Rents for Multinational Banking Activities (Onshore)

| Source of economic rents | Deposit taking (onshore) | Deposit taking (offshore) | Wholesale lending (local currency) | Wholesale lending (foreign currencies) | Syndicated lending | Project financing | Consumer lending | Foreign exchange trading | Total frequency |
|---|---|---|---|---|---|---|---|---|---|
| | Primary banking activity | | | | | | | | |
| 1. Size of a bank's total capital | | | 2 | 3 | 1 | | | | 6 |
| 2. Domestic(U.S.A.) U.S. dollar deposit base | | | 7 | 8 | 3 | | | | 18 |
| 3. Experiences & knowledge of multinational banking | | | | 3 | | 2 | | 3 | 8 |
| 4. Years of operations in the host markets | 5 | | 5 | | 3 | | | | 13 |
| 5. Breadth of multinational branch network | | | | | | | | 1 | 1 |
| 6. Availability of trained personnel(int'l officers) | | | | 3 | 5 | 3 | | 9 | 20 |
| 7. Effective interest rates differentials between host and home countries | | | 7 | 6 | | | | 1 | 14 |
| 8. Effective tax rates differentials between host and home countries | | | | | | | | | |
| 9. Size of the host country trade with the home country | 1 | | | 7 | | | | 1 | 9 |

Table 5-5 (continued)

| | Deposit taking (onshore) | Deposit taking (offshore) | Wholesale lending (local currency) | Wholesale lending (foreign currencies) | Syndicated lending | Project financing | Consumer lending | Foreign exchange trading | Total frequency |
|---|---|---|---|---|---|---|---|---|---|
| 10. Size of the home country direct investment in the host country | 5 | | 8 | 6 | | | | | 19 |
| 11. Size of the host country total foreign trade | | | 2 | 7 | 1 | | | 5 | 15 |
| 12. Size and depth of the host banking market | 2 | | 4 | 4 | 2 | 1 | | 1 | 14 |
| 13. Host country banking regulations | | | 1 | 1 | | | | | 2 |
| 14. Nationality of a bank | | | | | 1 | | | 2 | 3 |
| 15. Availability and ease of intra-bank transactions | | | 1 | 7 | 3 | 1 | | 4 | 16 |
| 16. Breadth of offshore network | | | | 3 | 2 | | | | 5 |
| 17. Availability and extensiveness of internal information control system | | | | | 4 | 1 | | 8 | 13 |
| Total Frequency | 13 | — | 37 | 58 | 25 | 8 | — | 35 | |

Note: Number indicates the degree of frequency a specific source is indicated as important for a specific banking activity.

**Summary of the Empirical Tests**

The test results show that the size of a bank is the most important ownership advantage in the case of U.S. MNBs. It is invariably related to other ownership advantage factors. Larger banks tend to have a dominant position in almost all aspects of ownership advantage. They tend to have more extensive domestic deposit bases, wider multinational banking networks, more experience in and technology of multinational banking, and well-developed and extensive intrabank funding facilities. Multinational banking is really a game of size. This explains why multinational banking has been dominated by a number of big banks.

Location advantages are also found to be important for the growth of MNBs. The net effects of location advantages are negative for the growth of MNBs. This is not surprising, considering the fact that banking is basically a regulated industry and the level of regulation is generally higher for foreign banks than for local banks. However, whether the net effects of location advantages are negative in both onshore and offshore markets or in either one of them is not clear. The net effects of location advantages are found to be favorable for the profitability of MNBs. This seems to imply that host governments are more concerned with preventing foreign dominance of local banking markets than limiting the earnings of foreign branches. The effects of individual location advantage factors are different among banking activities and between two host markets. Among various individual location advantages, size of a host banking market, size of home country trade with host countries, and size of home FDI in host countries are found to be highly correlated. In the onshore market (Korea), the lending rate differential, foreign exchange rate changes, and the size of the host banking market are instrumental to the growth of total assets of U.S. MNB branches, while the lending rate differential is significantly related to the growth of U.S. MNB branch lending. Both foreign exchange rate changes and the size of the host banking market are important for the growth of deposits accepted in foreign branches of U.S. MNBs.

In the offshore banking market (Singapore), no individual location advantages are found to be significantly related to the growth of U.S. MNB branches. This implies that the host offshore market has not provided U.S. MNBs with any significantly favorable location advantages compared to the U.S. market.

The tests produce inconclusive results with regard to the relation between individual location advantages and the branch profitability in both markets. The possibility of arbitrary realization (or removal) of profits in (or from) the books of MNB branches to maximize their global profits during the test periods may be one explanation for such results.

Finally, availability and ease of internal transactions is another important determinant of MNB growth. Transactions via internal channels can often reduce transaction costs unavoidable in external markets. This is more pronounced in information transactions, which are a major feature of multinational banking and the banking industry in general. The existence of extensive and efficient internal markets enables MNBs to scan worldwide business opportunities, to reduce costs of some transactions, and to move funds quickly for their most efficient use.

In the next chapter, specific examples of the activities of the most dominant group of MNBs (U.S. MNBs) in different banking environments are presented to highlight the findings and conclusions of this chapter. Due to the scarcity of necessary information and the parsimony of individual U.S. banks and their host banking authorities in disclosing more than minimally required information—mostly for reasons of confidentiality and unavailability—a full-scale examination of the case of individual banks is impossible. U.S. MNB activities in both offshore and onshore banking markets are studied with their experiences in Singapore and Korea, which are by no means representative, but which are the only markets where some information about U.S. bank branch activities is available in the Asia Pacific region. In other interesting markets of the region, such as Hong Kong and Taiwan, the host's banking regulation and disclosure requirements prevent the attainment of any useful information on individual U.S. bank branches. The activities of U.S. MNBs in the two countries are studied in terms of the three kinds of advantage necessary for MNBs—ownership advantage, location advantage, and internalization advantage—discussed in previous chapters.

## 6

# U.S. Multinational Banking Operations in the Asia Pacific Region

### Characteristics of U.S. Banking Activities in the Region

The U.S. banking presence in the Asia Pacific region was dominated by the big three—Bank of America, Citibank, and Chase Manhattan Bank—until recently. Citibank (formerly First National City Bank of New York) first opened its office in Singapore as early as 1902, but a more observable U.S. banking presence can be said to have begun in the early 1960s when the region began to engage in more active economic relations with other regions. However, a full-scale banking presence in the region had not occurred until the mid-1970s, although some banks were active in the offshore market before then. Major U.S. banks opened their offshore branches in Singapore in 1973 when offshore licenses were first issued. In Hong Kong and Korea, the full-scale banking presence is a more recent phenomenon, since only in 1978 did these countries begin to relax their selective closed-door policies toward foreign banks. Table 6-1 shows the number of U.S. MNBs with branches in four major countries of the region since 1970. In this section, the state of U.S. banking presence in the region and the major operational attributes of U.S. banks there will be explained to promote a general understanding of the banking environments in the region before investigating how location advantages affect the patterns of MNB activities in foreign host markets.

Unlike MNBs of non-U.S. nationality, U.S. MNBs have the intrinsic advantage of having easier access to the major vehicle currency source. As the U.S. dollar has been the most important international vehicle currency since World War II, U.S. banks with their extensive U.S. dollar deposit base have dominated multinational banking. This phenomenon has been especially remarkable in the Asia Pacific region, since the region has been traditionally a net borrower of major international vehicle currencies. However, the dominant position of U.S. banks there has experienced a relative contraction recently. In 1976, U.S. MNBs provided about 70 percent of the total publicized syndicated

Table 6-1.   Number of U.S. MNBs[1] with Branches in
the Asia Pacific Region

|  | Singapore[2] | Hong Kong | Korea | Taiwan |
|---|---|---|---|---|
| 1970 | 4(4) | 3 | 3 | 2 |
| 1971 | 4(4) | 3 | 3 | 2 |
| 1972 | 4(4) | 3 | 3 | 3 |
| 1973 | 8(4) | 3 | 3 | 5 |
| 1974 | 11(4) | 3 | 3 | 7 |
| 1975 | 15(4) | 3 | 3 | 7 |
| 1976 | 16(4) | 3 | 3 | 7 |
| 1977 | 17(4) | 3 | 4 | 7 |
| 1978 | 17(4) | 5 | 5 | 7 |
| 1979 | 17(4) | 9 | 9 | 9 |
| 1980 | 20(4) | 12 | 9 | 10 |
| 1983 | 25(4) | 22 | 13 | 12 |

1. American Express Corporation (AMEX) is not included.
2. Number of banks with full licenses in parentheses.

Source:   *Polk's World Bank Directory,* various issues.
*Rand McNally International Bankers Directory,* various issues.
Lee, S.Y. and Y.C. Jao, *Financial Structures and Monetary Policies in Southeast Asia* (New York: St. Martin's Press, 1982).

credit commitments to the region, but this figure fell to about 20 percent in 1979. The relative decline was accompanied by a threefold increase in the market share of European banks, and a tenfold increase by Japanese banks. This is because some relative newcomers to this market have embarked on the age-old practice of buying market share by cutting price.[1] For many banks, profitability is not the only criterion by which they make a decision to lend. Some banks are content with lower profitability expectations as a general policy; others make a conscious decision to trade profitability for market share, cementing a relationship, supporting a home country national objective, and so on. Some banks are influenced principally by overall return on assets, and do not consider spread alone as the significant factor. Besides, the strategic considerations of borrowers to diversify funding sources by bank, country, and type of instrument also are responsible for the relative setback of U.S. banks in the region. However, this setback in relative U.S. market share of a rapidly growing overall market could simply be a reflection of a catching-up process entered into by banks from other industrialized countries as well as major countries in the region.[2] Nevertheless, U.S. MNBs remain the dominant power in the region.

Several attributes of the operations of U.S. MNBs in the region can be noted. First, big money-center banks have been most active. Major banks from New York and San Francisco have dominated both the offshore and onshore banking markets of the region. Until 1978, no regional banks had branch offices in the onshore banking markets of Singapore, Hong Kong, Korea, or Taiwan, with the exception of the First Interstate Bank of California (formerly United California Bank) in Taiwan. In the offshore banking market of Singapore, some regional banks and medium-size money-center banks did, however, open their offshore branches as early as 1973. Bank size seems to play an important role in U.S. MNBs' multinational expansion into the region, especially their expansion into the relatively new onshore market.

Second, the Asia Pacific region has been and continues to be one of the most profitable areas of the world for major U.S. banks (table 6-2). Since the 1970s, no serious case of default or rescheduling problems of sovereign lending has occurred in the region,[3] though three of the eight LDCs with the largest borrowings, Korea, the Philippines and Indonesia, are in the region.[4] This has been mainly due to the region's continuously growing demands for external loans, relatively less competitive banking markets than Western Europe, the predominantly wholesale nature of the business, and the relatively higher interest rates of the region.

Third, the involvement of U.S. MNBs in the region has gradually increased compared with other regions, particularly with respect to Europe which had long been the major market for U.S. MNBs. Table 6-3 shows one aspect of this phenomenon. The share of assets committed to the Asia Pacific region has increased gradually for most major banks. Rapidly growing economies in this region, as well as relatively stagnant economies and excessive competition in traditional multinational banking markets of Europe, seem to be the prime reasons for this. In addition, many second-tier money-center banks and regional banks have found expansion into the Asia Pacific region less costly and easier to accommodate in their global objectives than expansion into the traditional markets. The phenomenon implies the importance of market opportunities (location advantages) for MNB growth. The market opportunities of some countries of the region will be detailed later.

Fourth, one can observe a remarkable presence of second-tier money-center banks and regional banks in the Asia Pacific region since 1974. Difficulties of U.S. domestic expansion due to regulations and the sluggish domestic economy, the removal of U.S. regulations on capital outflow,[5] increased U.S. trade with the region, increased U.S. direct investment in the region, the development of new offshore financial markets in the region, and

Table 6-2. Profitability (ROA)[1] of Multinational Operations of Selected U.S. Banks by Region

| | 1977 (%) | | | | 1978 (%) | | | | 1980 (%) | | | | 1983 (%) | | | |
|---|---|---|---|---|---|---|---|---|---|---|---|---|---|---|---|---|
| | Asia Pacific | Europe | South & Central America | Total | Asia Pacific | Europe | South & Central American | Total | Asia Pacific | Europe | South & Central America | Total | Asia Pacific | Europe | South & Central American | Total |
| Bank of America | 1.13 | 0.78 | 1.38 | 0.99 | 1.03 | 0.87 | 0.85 | 0.97 | 1.81 | 0.78 | 1.20 | 1.22 | 0.82 | 0.83[2] | (0.48) | 0.59 |
| Citicorp | 0.74 | 0.93 | 3.86 | 1.30 | 0.92 | 0.89 | 3.35 | 1.26 | 1.55[2] | 0.07 | 1.33 | 0.79 | 1.54 | 1.14[2] | 0.26 | 0.67 |
| Chase Manhattan | 0.96 | 0.60 | 0.08 | 0.61 | 0.95 | 0.50 | 0.56 | 0.67 | 1.15 | 0.52 | 0.51 | 0.71 | 0.59 | 0.25 | 0.85[3] | 0.58 |
| Manufacturers Hanover | 1.37 | 1.29 | 1.32 | 1.23 | 0.94[2] | 0.74 | 1.59 | 1.02 | 0.81 | 0.70 | 0.86 | 0.77 | 0.52[2] | 1.09 | 1.39 | 1.06 |
| J.P. Morgan | 1.32 | 1.13 | 1.44 | 1.23 | 1.02 | 1.10 | 1.63 | 1.20 | 1.26 | 1.51 | 1.89 | 1.56 | 1.52 | 1.82 | 1.27 | 1.60 |
| First Chicago | 0.62 | 0.26 | 0.91 | 0.56 | 0.67 | (0.03) | 1.89 | 0.07 | 1.15 | 0.52 | 0.51 | 0.71 | (0.23) | (0.04) | 0.40 | 0.16 |
| Continental Illinois | 0.20 | 0.30 | 1.05 | 0.23 | 0 | 0.64 | 0.38 | 0.45 | 0.31 | 0.89 | 0.97 | 0.86 | 0.03 | 0.45 | (1.01) | 0.10 |
| Bank of New York | N.A. | | | | 0.52 | 0.43 | 0.49 | 0.46 | 0.41 | 0.57 | 0.50 | 0.52 | 0.50 | 0.73 | 0.61 | 0.65 |

1. Income before tax/total assets.
2. Middle East and Africa included.
3. Canada included.

Note:  New accounting standards issued by the Financial Accounting Standards Board (FASB) in 1977 do not allow a comparison of ROAs prior to 1977 with those of 1977 and after.

Source:  Individual banks' annual reports and 10-K reports.

Table 6-3. Size of Assets of Overseas Operations of Selected U.S. Banks by Region (In million U.S. dollars)

| | 1977 (%) | | | | 1978 (%) | | | |
|---|---|---|---|---|---|---|---|---|
| | Asia Pacific | Europe | South & Central America | Total | Asia Pacific | Europe | South & Central America | Total |
| Bank of America | 5,408(16.33) | 20,129(60.78) | 3,247(9.80) | 33,116(100%) | 6,205 (17.18) | 21,574(59.73) | 3,900(10.80) | 36,118(100%) |
| Citicorp | 7,165(17.24) | 18,432(44.36) | 4,664(11.22) | 41,548(100%) | 8,468 (16.63) | 23,849(46.83) | 5,454(10.71) | 50,931(100%) |
| Chase Manhattan | 6,316(25.38) | 10,064(40.44) | 7,032(28.26) | 24,883(100%) | 6,398 (20.26) | 13,789(32.66) | 9,120(28.88) | 31,583(100%) |
| Manufacturers Hanover | 2,735(17.11) | 7,760(48.55) | 4,097(25.63) | 15,984(100%) | 4,343[1](23.08) | 9,654(51.31) | 4,524(24.04) | 18,814(100%) |
| J.P. Morgan | 2,035(12.19) | 10,515(62.98) | 3,466(20.76) | 16,695(100%) | 3,116 (14.63) | 13,136(61.69) | 3,820(17.94) | 21,295(100%) |
| First Chicago | 848(10.40) | 1,793(21.99) | 1,379(16.92) | 8,152(100%) | 831 (9.85) | 1,879(22.27) | 988(11.71) | 8,438(100%) |
| Continental Illinois | 979(9.48) | 4,604(44.60) | 1,234(11.96) | 10,322(100%) | 1,500(15.46) | 3,600(37.11) | 1,600(16.49) | 9,700(100%) |
| Bank of New York | N.A. | | | | 446 (17.82) | 1,383(55.25) | 575(22.97) | 2,503(100%) |
| All U.S. Member Banks | 29,126[2] (12.78) | 115,201 (50.56) | 73,254 (32.15) | 227,868 (100%) | 32,163 (12.49) | 128,781 (49.99) | 82,481 (32.02) | 257,580 (100%) |

Table 6-3 (continued)

| | 1980 (%) | | | | 1983 (%) | | | |
|---|---|---|---|---|---|---|---|---|
| | Asia Pacific | Europe | South & Central America | Total | Asia Pacific | Europe | South & Central America | Total |
| Bank of America | 9,019 (20.35) | 24,878(56.14) | 5,581(12.59) | 44,311(100%) | 12,385 (25.08) | 22,924[1](46.42) | 8,548 (17.31) | 49,381(100%) |
| Citicorp | 18,226[1](17.02) | 31,434(29.35) | 16,400(15.31) | 107,094(100%) | 22,438 (17.54) | 30,461[1](23.81) | 18,516 (14.47) | 127,923(100%) |
| Chase Manhattan | 8,504 (21.18) | 16,393(40.84) | 12,993(32.37) | 40,141(100%) | 12,400 (26.75) | 16,150 (34.84) | 14,260[3](30.76) | 46,350(100%) |
| Manufacturers Hanover | 6,207 (22.04) | 13,796(48.98) | 7,224(25.65) | 28,165(100%) | 6,723[1](23.10) | 12,656 (43.49) | 8,846 (30.40) | 29,101(100%) |
| J.P. Morgan | 4,716 (17.27) | 16,116(59.01) | 5,338(19.54) | 27,312(100%) | 5,141 (16.78) | 16,683 (54.44) | 7,220 (23.56) | 30,642(100%) |
| First Chicago | 1,916 (15.46) | 2,880(23.23) | 1,401(11.30) | 12,395(100%) | 2,500 (18.46) | 5,504 (40.64) | 2,518 (18.59) | 13,542(100%) |
| Continental Illinois | 1,951 (14.96) | 7,312(56.06) | 2,377(18.22) | 13,043(100%) | 3,069 (21.35) | 6,699 (46.60) | 2,966 (20.63) | 14,375(100%) |
| Bank of New York | 636 (22.29) | 1,499(52.54) | 701(24.57) | 2,853(100%) | 478 (15.95) | 1,473 (49.15) | 911 (30.40) | 2,997(100%) |
| All U.S. Member Banks | 46,211[2](13.45) | 170,474(49.63) | 112,815(32.86) | 343,461(100%) | 70,456[2](18.31) | 119,834(31.14) | 45,204(11.74) | 384,856(100%) |

1. Middle East and Africa included.
2. Middle East included.
3. Canada included.

Source:    Individual banks' annual reports and 10-K reports.
Assets and Liabilities of Overseas Branches, Member Banks of the Federal Reserve System (Board of Governors of the Federal Reserve System Press Release).

the long-term potential of the region, especially with the opening of China, seem to have set off the expansion of second-tier money-center banks into the region. Table 6-4 shows the state of involvement of such banks in the region.

Table 6-4.    Regional Origin of U.S. MNBs with
Branches in Four Major Countries[1] in
the Asia Pacific Region

|      | N.Y. | Calif. | Illinois | Texas | Mass. | Wash. | Penn. | N. Caro-lina | Mich. | N.J. | Washing-ton D.C. | R.I. |
|------|------|--------|----------|-------|-------|-------|-------|------|-------|------|------|------|
| 1970 | 2 | 1 | 1 | 0 | 0 | 0 | 0 | 0 | 0 | 0 | 0 | 0 |
| 1971 | 2 | 1 | 1 | 0 | 0 | 0 | 0 | 0 | 0 | 0 | 0 | 0 |
| 1972 | 2 | 1 | 1 | 0 | 0 | 0 | 0 | 0 | 0 | 0 | 0 | 0 |
| 1973 | 5 | 1 | 2 | 1 | 0 | 0 | 0 | 0 | 0 | 0 | 0 | 0 |
| 1974 | 7 | 2 | 2 | 1 | 0 | 0 | 0 | 0 | 0 | 0 | 0 | 0 |
| 1975 | 9 | 2 | 2 | 2 | 0 | 0 | 0 | 0 | 0 | 0 | 0 | 0 |
| 1976 | 9 | 2 | 2 | 2 | 0 | 1 | 0 | 0 | 0 | 0 | 0 | 0 |
| 1977 | 9 | 3 | 2 | 2 | 0 | 1 | 0 | 0 | 0 | 0 | 0 | 0 |
| 1978 | 9 | 3 | 3 | 2 | 0 | 1 | 0 | 0 | 0 | 0 | 0 | 0 |
| 1979 | 9 | 3 | 3 | 2 | 1 | 1 | 0 | 1 | 0 | 0 | 0 | 0 |
| 1980 | 10 | 4 | 4 | 2 | 1 | 2 | 1 | 1 | 0 | 0 | 0 | 0 |
| 1983 | 10 | 7 | 4 | 3 | 3 | 3 | 2 | 1 | 2 | 1 | 1 | 1 |

1. Singapore, Hong Kong, Taiwan, and Korea.

Source:   See Table 6-1.

Finally, the principal type of business conducted by U.S. banks in the region is of the wholesale nature. U.S. banks are more actively engaged in Eurodollar deposits and lending, dollar-swap lending, interbank transactions, foreign exchange trading, and acceptance finance than in local deposit gathering and retail lending. This seems to be natural for them, as they have comparative advantages (ownership advantages) over local banks in conducting these activities. With an extensive dollar deposit base, experience and skills gleaned from operating in sophisticated financial markets, and expertise in foreign exchange trading, they are more likely to outcompete their local counterparts in these lines of business than in local deposit gathering and retail lending, which need an extensive local network and market familiarity.

With these general observations, this chapter will investigate the operations of U.S. MNB branches in the two major banking markets of the region for which consistent data are available. The objective is to obtain an understanding of how location advantages affect the patterns of banking activities in the foreign host market. It appears that once MNBs enter a certain foreign market, the patterns of their banking activities seem to be formed largely by the location advantages of the foreign market. Thus, it is hypothesized that the patterns of banking activity of branches of different MNBs (banks which thus possess different ownership and internalization advantages) in a certain foreign market are more similar than those of branches of the same MNB (possessing the same ownership and internalization advantages) operating in different foreign markets. This may be primarily due to one major characteristic of the banking industry, the relatively limited scope of product differentiability and innovation. Under such conditions, a bank's ownership advantages may be better exploited in reinforcing economies of scale advantages in existing products, rather than in product differentiation and innovation. With limited types of product available and relatively standard and known production processes, the selection of products to be produced may be influenced more by the market opportunities of specific products than by the bank's ability to produce them efficiently, as standardized products generally would not provide much room for efficiency improvement. This would be more pronounced among MNBs, since MNBs generally have more than a necessary level of ownership advantages needed for the efficient production of standardized banking products.

The four banking markets of Singapore, Hong Kong, Taiwan, and Korea provide a very useful setting for observing multinational banking activities from two different perspectives. Singapore's offshore market and Hong Kong's banking industry are relatively unregulated, while Taiwanese and Korean banking markets are highly regulated. In addition, U.S. MNBs have been the most conspicuous presence in these markets in the region, in addition to Japan. Although Japan provides sizable banking markets, her well-entrenched domestic banking industry, domestic market competition, and relatively restrictive environment have shifted the attention of most MNBs toward these other rapidly expanding banking markets. However, in the case of Hong Kong and Taiwan, no significant and consistent information on U.S. MNB activities is available, due either to liberal disclosure requirements (Hong Kong) or to host government ordinances on banking secrecy (Taiwan). Thus, this investigation will center on the activities of U.S. MNBs in Singapore and Korea, which still provide a very useful setting for study, to see if their banking activities are similar within a given host market and different between the two host markets.

## U.S. Multinational Banking Operations in Singapore

*The Commercial Banking Markets in Singapore*

*Characteristics of the commercial banking markets.* Two separate banking markets coexist in Singapore, the onshore domestic banking market and the offshore Asian currency market. The two markets are characterized by differences in participating banks, governing regulations, and major types of business conducted. Commercial banks need a special license from the Monetary Authority of Singapore (M.A.S.) to operate in the offshore market—the so-called Asian Currency Unit (ACU) license. Only full license and restricted license banks are authorized to conduct banking operations in the onshore domestic market. Transactions in the offshore market are given a number of fiscal and banking incentives and exemptions—for example, exemption from exchange control, no withholding tax on interest income from nonresident foreign currency deposits, no reserve requirements with the M.A.S., no liquidity requirements, and lower corporate tax on net income from offshore activities. The two markets also differ in terms of currency, size, and nature. In this section, the onshore domestic commercial banking market of Singapore will be studied. The offshore banking market will be discussed in the next section.

One of the major characteristics of Singapore's commercial banking market is its bank licensing system. Under the Banking Act of 1970, the M.A.S. issues three different types of banking license—full license, restricted license, and offshore license. Full license banks are authorized to transact the whole range of commercial banking business. Activities open to full license banks include the acceptance of current, savings, and time deposits, the financing of exports and imports, the transfer of funds, commercial letters of credit, trust receipts, the purchase and sale of traveler's checks and currencies, and other related banking activities. Restricted license banks may engage in banking business in the same way as the full license banks except that: (1) they are not permitted to accept time deposits of less than S$250,000; (2) they may not operate savings accounts; and (3) they may not operate at more than one location in Singapore. Offshore license banks were permitted to concentrate only on business outside Singapore when offshore licenses were first introduced in 1973. Thus they were authorized to operate Asian Currency Units (ACUs)—an operational entity for offshore banking—and to deal in foreign exchange, but not to offer current, savings, or time deposit facilities. They could transact business in Singapore only with banks and other approved financial institutions. They were not allowed to deal with resident nonbank customers except in transactions specified in the M.A.S. guidelines. However, following the June 1978 liberalization of exchange control most of these restrictions were relaxed and the only limit is that the total amount loaned to a Singapore resident must not exceed S$30 million at any one time.[6] Offshore license banks may now provide current accounts, overdrafts, trust receipts, and letters of credit to Singapore residents. As of the end of 1982, there were 37 full license banks (13 domestic banks and 24 foreign banks), 13 restricted license banks (all foreign banks), and 68 offshore license banks (all foreign banks) in Singapore (table 6-5). All offshore license banks and some of the full and restricted license banks are given permission to operate ACU accounts in the offshore market.

The bank licensing system aims to protect Singapore from an excessive number of banks operating in the domestic banking market, which could crowd out small local banks operating on a modest capital base. Furthermore, it aims to limit access to the offshore market to well-established foreign and domestic banks of medium to large size.[7] Since the enactment of the Banking Act of 1970, only three full licenses have been issued and no restricted licenses

Table 6-5.   Number and Types of Commercial Banks
in Singapore, 1970-1982

| | Domestic | Foreign | | | Total | |
|---|---|---|---|---|---|---|
| Year | Full License | Full License | Restricted License | Offshore License | Number of Banks | Foreign Rep. Offices |
| 1970 | 11 | 26 | – | – | 37 | 8 |
| 1971 | 11 | 25 | 6 | – | 42 | 19 |
| 1972 | 11 | 25 | 8 | – | 44 | 27 |
| 1973 | 11 | 25 | 12 | 7 | 54 | 30 |
| 1974 | 12 | 24 | 12 | 14 | 62 | 36 |
| 1975 | 13 | 24 | 12 | 21 | 70 | 38 |
| 1976 | 13 | 24 | 12 | 23 | 72 | 40 |
| 1977 | 13 | 24 | 13 | 27 | 77 | 43 |
| 1978 | 13 | 24 | 13 | 31 | 81 | 44 |
| 1979 | 13 | 24 | 13 | 39 | 89 | 47 |
| 1980 | 13 | 24 | 13 | 47 | 97 | 49 |
| 1982 | 13 | 24 | 13 | 68 | 118 | 55 |

Source:    Monetary Authority of Singapore, *Annual Reports,* various issues.

have been issued to local banks. Since 1973, only offshore banking licenses have been granted—all to foreign banks. This shows that the policy of the M.A.S. has been to limit new foreign banks to those areas of local business in which their operations are complementary to, rather than competitive with, the operations of the local and fully licensed banks. As for the expected future development of this policy, one study implied that full and restricted licenses would be issued only under exceptional circumstances as "the general opinion is that Singapore is already 'fully-banked' in so far as domestic banking is concerned."[8]

A second major characteristic of the Singapore onshore market is the movement among domestic banks toward internationalization. Domestic banks have increased their global contacts and reinforced the international relations originally established through trade links. Leading domestic banks have set up branches or representative offices in other financial centers and major cities in the region. However, their Malaysian operations still constitute their single largest business outside Singapore. Increasing reliance of the Singapore commercial banking system on external funding sources also shows this trend toward internationalization. Not only have transactions with banks abroad increased remarkably, but the system has increasingly drawn finances from abroad. A net balance due to banks abroad increased from S$115.3 million in 1970 to S$4,389.1 million in 1982. Part of the balance is due to banks in the Asian currency market, but the majority of it comes from foreign banks outside Singapore. Of the 1982 net balance of S$4,389.1 million, S$609.3 million was due to banks in the Asian currency market whereas S$3,779.3 million was to foreign banks outside Singapore.

Third, the market can be characterized as a dynamic and rapidly growing one. The size of the commercial banking system, measured by total assets, increased from S$5,042 million in 1970 to S$48,537 million in 1982, an annual average rate of 21 percent (table 6-6). The growth was faster than that of the nominal GDP during the same period, which sustained an annual average growth rate of 14.5 percent on a current market price basis. Loans and advances grew from S$2,722 million in 1970 to S$29,443 million in 1982, which is equivalent to an average annual rate of 22 percent growth. Deposits of nonbank customers grew by seven times during the period from 1970 to 1982 which is an average annual growth of 18 percent. Capital and reserves, which were related to domestic banks only, because foreign banks had their capital reserves on a global basis, increased by fifteen times during the period, equivalent to 25 percent annual growth. Such growth rates are quite remarkable, even allowing for the effects of inflation.

The growth in the magnitude of the market has accompanied an enhancement of the quality of the market. The higher growth rate of capital funds than that of deposits signifies the high profitability of banks and also the

Table 6-6. Assets and Liabilities of Commercial Banks in Singapore, 1970-1982 (End of year, in million Singapore dollars)

| | 1970 | 1973 | 1976 | 1979 | 1980 | 1982 |
|---|---|---|---|---|---|---|
| **LIABILITIES:** | | | | | | |
| Paid-up capital and reserves* | 292.3 | 787.7 | 1,270.9 | 1,861.2 | 2,665.4 | 4,301.3 |
| Deposits of nonbank customers | 3,194.9 | 5,799.8 | 8,488.5 | 12,178.4 | 16,035.0 | 23,408.7 |
| Demand deposits | 947.7 | 1,786.2 | 2,378.2 | 3,244.3 | 3,484.0 | 4,781.4 |
| Fixed deposits | 1,818.3 | 3,264.8 | 5,062.4 | 7,473.0 | 10,788.4 | 15,619.7 |
| Savings deposits | 412.9 | 708.5 | 999.2 | 1,394.8 | 1,692.5 | 2,917.4 |
| Other deposits | 16.0 | 40.3 | 48.7 | 66.3 | 70.1 | 90.2 |
| Amounts due to banks | 1,045.8 | 3,063.0 | 4,432.0 | 8,615.9 | 9,942.5 | 14,426.4 |
| In Singapore | 599.5 | 964.9 | 1,372.2 | 2,415.4 | 2,888.4 | 3,941.6 |
| Outside Singapore†† | 446.3 | 2,098.1 | 3,059.8 | 6,200.5 | 7,054.1 | 10,484.8 |
| S$NCD issued | – | – | 617.8 | 515.0 | 313.9 | 428.0 |
| Other liabilities | 469.0 | 1,068.8 | 1,717.6 | 3,577.3 | 4,341.3 | 5,972.8 |
| Total assets/liabilities | 5,041.6 | 10,719.3 | 16,526.8 | 26,747.8 | 33,316.1 | 48,537.2 |
| **ASSETS:** | | | | | | |
| Cash | 43.3 | 70.4 | 105.3 | 161.1 | 272.4 | 247.9 |
| Balance with M.A.S. | 129.0 | 593.9 | 511.7 | 733.7 | 923.1 | 1,417.5 |
| Money at call with discount houses | – | 354.5 | 491.4 | 695.7 | 884.1 | 1,917.9 |
| Treasury bills | 596.0 | 340.0 | 328.5 | 369.9 | 688.9 | 568.4 |
| S$NCDs held | – | – | 380.1 | 166.2 | 127.8 | 76.8 |
| Amounts due from banks | 940.8 | 1,746.5 | 3,528.7 | 5,646.6 | 6,880.1 | 9,823.6 |
| In Singapore | 609.8 | 874.1 | 1,370.5 | 1,986.6 | 2,756.7 | 3,727.9 |
| Outside Singapore†† | 331.0 | 872.4 | 2,158.2 | 3,660.0 | 4,123.4 | 6,095.7 |
| Investments: | | | | | | |
| In Singapore | 232.0 | 727.0 | 1,365.7 | 1,639.6 | 1,845.7 | 2,994.4 |
| Goverment Securities | 90.3 | 333.0 | 762.0 | 908.9 | 861.1 | 1,016.2 |
| Other securities† | 142.0 | 394.0 | 603.7 | 730.7 | 984.6 | 1,978.2 |
| Outside Singapore | 93.1 | 90.0 | 81.1 | 51.0 | 69.2 | 123.6 |
| Loans and advances to nonbank customers | 2,167.7 | 5,146.5 | 7,271.7 | 12,058.7 | 16,157.5 | 25,335.6 |
| Bills discounted or purchased | 554.4 | 1,124.7 | 1,622.5 | 3,948.3 | 4,049.4 | 4,107.3 |
| Other assets | 285.0 | 525.8 | 840.1 | 1,277.0 | 1,417.9 | 1,924.2 |

* Refer to local banks only.

† Other securities include loans of public authorities, private company stocks, and equity investment.

†† Amounts due to banks and amounts due from banks outside Singapore include Asian Currency Units.

Source: Monetary Authority of Singapore, *Annual Reports*, 1972-1982/83; *Quarterly Bulletin*, 1973-1983.

adequacy of capital funds in the banking system. The deposit structure also has been improved, as time and savings deposits grew faster than demand deposits (table 6-7). The liquidity ratio of the commercial banking system, which is the ratio of liquid assets[9] to deposits of nonbank customers, increased gradually from 0.41 in 1970 to 0.6 in 1982. This liquidity ratio should be considered high by international standards.[10]

Table 6-7.   Types of Deposits of Commercial Banks in Singapore (In million Singapore dollars)

| Deposits | 1970 | 1973 | 1976 | 1979 | 1980 | 1982 |
|---|---|---|---|---|---|---|
| Demand | 947.7 | 1,786.2 | 2,378.2 | 3,244.3 | 3,484.0 | 4,781.4 |
| Fixed | 1,818.3 | 3,264.8 | 5,062.4 | 7,473.0 | 10,788.4 | 15,619.7 |
| Savings | 412.9 | 708.5 | 999.2 | 1,394.8 | 1,692.5 | 2,917.4 |
| Others | 16.0 | 40.3 | 48.7 | 66.3 | 70.1 | 90.2 |
| Total | 3,194.9 | 5,799.8 | 8,488.5 | 12,178.4 | 16,035.0 | 23,408.7 |

Source:   Monetary Authority of Singapore, *Annual Reports,* 1972-1982/83; *Quarterly Bulletin,* 1973-1983.

Finally, one can observe a gradual deregulatory trend in the Singapore domestic onshore banking market since the midseventies. Abolition of the cartel system of determining interest rates and the dismantling of foreign exchange controls are the most significant features of this trend. When the cartel system of interest rates determination was abolished in July 1975, banks were left free to quote their own rates of interest.[11] Before then, interest rates had been determined by the agreements of member banks of the Association of Banks in Singapore, in consultation with the M.A.S. The freeing of interest rates has brought competition into the market, and has forced individual banks to pay more attention to efficient asset and liability management.

The abolition of foreign exchange controls in 1978 allowed foreign banks with offshore licenses to participate in the domestic onshore banking market. This was equivalent to an indirect relaxation of Singapore's stringent policies on entry into the domestic market. In addition, it helped to bring the two separate banking markets closer and thus nurtured dynamism and innovation in what otherwise might have been stagnant and dull domestic banking markets.

However, Singapore still takes a very restrictive position on the issue of branching. Only full license banks can operate in multiple locations, and only three full licenses have been issued since 1970. Other than this, Singapore, like most countries, retains various banking acts, regulations, and guidelines to ensure her banks' capital adequacy, liquidity, and prudence in portfolios.[12]

*The Asian currency market.* The Asian currency market was initially set up as an intermediary between several national capital markets and the Eurocurrency market, as were a number of other offshore financial centers in the late 1960s. In most cases, the activity of such offshore markets was limited to intermediation between major neighboring countries which restricted international movements of capital, and the Eurocurrency market, as was the case in the Caribbean offshore markets. However, the Asian currency market went beyond this function, and has now developed a substantial regional network of financial transactions. It provides an arbitrage function between markets in Asia, the Middle East, and Europe, serves as a major avenue for channeling funds into development projects in many Asian countries, and acts as an efficient medium for mobilizing these countries' surplus funds and for placing them elsewhere in the region.

The Asian currency market was created through the deliberate action of the Singapore government which, in response to an important transition in its economy, wished to develop the country as an international financial center. Since independence in 1965, Singapore has tried to expand financial and trade relations to countries other than the British Commonwealth and the immediate neighboring countries. Thus, the creation of the market can be seen as a part of this transition toward more diversified economic ties. [13]

Since its inception, the market has grown remarkably. As of March 1983, there were 153 Asian Currency Units (106 commercial banks, 45 merchant banks, and 2 investment companies). The size of the market, measured by its total assets, grew from US$31 million in 1968, to US$12,597 million in 1975 and to US$103,295 million in 1982 (table 6-8). Compared with the Eurocurrency market, the Asian currency market is still small but, due to the rapid growth (table 6-9) of that market, Singapore has firmly established itself as a key financial center in Asia. Unlike a lot of tax-haven loan booking centers, which are not backed up by the real economy, Singapore is a real market, with a small but healthy domestic financial market. The reasons for this success are many, among them being: (1) Singapore is situated in the middle of the fast-growing ASEAN (Association of Southeast-Asian Nations) region and in a strategic time zone linking the U.S., Europe, and Japan; (2) Singapore has political stability, a strong domestic economy, and a stable currency; (3) it has well-developed physical and financial infrastructures and transportation and communications facilities; (4) it has sufficient administrative and technical expertise to introduce timely measures to boost the market; and (5) various international financial institutions have responded to these conditions by setting up operations in Singapore.

The market derives its funds from and lends them to both banking and nonbanking sources. Major banking sources are central banks, commercial banks and other financial institutions. Nonbanking sources are mainly MNCs, government agencies, firms involved in international and regional trade, and

Table 6-8. Asian Currency Market: Assets and Liabilities of Asian Currency Units (In million U.S. dollars)

| End of Period | Assets | | | | | | Liabilities | | | | |
|---|---|---|---|---|---|---|---|---|---|---|---|
| | Loans to Nonbanks | Interbank Funds | | | Other Assets | Total Assets/ Liabilities | Deposits of Nonbanks | Interbank Funds | | | Other Liabilities |
| | | Total Interbank | In Singapore | Outside Singapore | | | | Total Interbank | In Singapore | Outside Singapore | |
| 1968 | 2 (5) | 29 (95) | n.a. - | n.a. - | negli. - | 31 (100) | 18 (58) | 13 (41) | n.a. - | n.a. - | negli. - |
| 1969 | 1 (1) | 121 (98) | n.a. - | n.a. - | 2 (1) | 123 (100) | 98 (80) | 24 (19) | n.a. - | n.a. - | 1 (1) |
| 1970 | 14 (4) | 370 (95) | 13 (3) | 357 (92) | 6 (2) | 390 (100) | 244 (63) | 141 (36) | 6 (1) | 135 (35) | 5 (1) |
| 1971 | 189 (18) | 851 (80) | 39 (4) | 812 (76) | 23 (2) | 1063 (100) | 238 (23) | 811 (76) | 56 (5) | 755 (71) | 14 (1) |
| 1972 | 601 (20) | 2331 (78) | 99 (4) | 2232 (75) | 44 (2) | 2976 (100) | 399 (13) | 2550 (86) | 145 (5) | 2405 (81) | 27 (1) |
| 1973 | 1214 (19) | 4962 (79) | 262 (4) | 4700 (75) | 101 (2) | 6277 (100) | 913 (15) | 5249 (84) | 406 (7) | 4844 (77) | 115 (2) |
| 1974 | 2629 (35) | 7528 (73) | 223 (2) | 7305 (71) | 200 (2) | 10357 (100) | 1614 (15) | 8531 (82) | 676 (7) | 7856 (76) | 212 (2) |

Table 6-8. (continued)

| | | Assets | | | | | | Liabilities | | | |
| | | Interbank Funds | | | | | | Interbank Funds | | | |
| End of Period | Loans to Nonbanks | Total Interbank | In Singapore | Outside Singapore | Other Assets | Total Assets/ Liabilities | Deposits of Nonbanks | Total Interbank | In Singapore | Outside Singapore | Other Liabilities |
|---|---|---|---|---|---|---|---|---|---|---|---|
| 1975 | 3303 (26) | 9099 (72) | 270 (2) | 8828 (70) | 196 (2) | 12597 (100) | 2068 (16) | 10294 (82) | 584 (5) | 9710 (77) | 235 (2) |
| 1976 | 4048 (23) | 12951 (75) | 414 (2) | 12537 (72) | 354 (2) | 17354 (100) | 1960 (11) | 15067 (87) | 799 (5) | 14268 (82) | 327 (2) |
| 1977 | 5281 (25) | 15253 (73) | 573 (3) | 14679 (70) | 485 (2) | 21018 (100) | 2255 (11) | 18350 (87) | 1382 (7) | 16968 (81) | 413 (2) |
| 1978 | 6377 (24) | 19830 (73) | 867 (3) | 18963 (70) | 834 (3) | 27040 (100) | 3600 (13) | 21987 (81) | 1443 (5) | 20545 (76) | 1453 (6) |
| 1979 | 8484 (22) | 28094 (74) | 1100 (3) | 26993 (71) | 1585 (4) | 38163 (100) | 5771 (15) | 29425 (77) | 1882 (5) | 27543 (72) | 2966 (8) |
| 1980 | 12402 (23) | 39552 (73) | 1085 (2) | 38467 (71) | 2438 (4) | 54392 (100) | 9322 (17) | 40879 (75) | 1304 (2) | 39575 (73) | 4191 (10) |
| 1982 | 27606 (27) | 69564 (62) | 1739 (2) | 67825 (65) | 6125 (6) | 103295 (100) | 17630 (17) | 79223 (77) | 1497 (2) | 77726 (75) | 6442 (7) |

Note: Figures in parentheses show percentages.

Source: Monetary Authority of Singapore. *Annual Reports.*

Table 6-9.   Comparison of Size of Eurocurrency Market and Asian
Currency Market (In million U.S. dollars)

| Year | Eurocurrency Market Size | Annual Increase (%) | Asian Currency Market Size | Annual Increase (%) | ACM as % of Euro-Market |
|------|-----------|-----|-----------|-----|-----|
| 1970 | 110,000 (65,000) | -( - ) | 390(334) | -( - ) | 0.4(0.5) |
| 1971 | 145,000 (85,000) | 32(31) | 1,063(950) | 173(184) | 0.7(1.1) |
| 1972 | 200,000(110,000) | 38(29) | 2,976(2,372) | 180(150) | 1.5(2.1) |
| 1973 | 315,000(160,000) | 58(45) | 6,277(4,577) | 111 (93) | 2.0(2.9) |
| 1974 | 395,000(220,000) | 25(38) | 10,357(8,212) | 65 (79) | 2.6(3.7) |
| 1975 | 485,000(255,000) | 23(16) | 12,597(10,224) | 22 (25) | 2.6(4.0) |
| 1976 | 595,000(320,000) | 23(25) | 17,354(14,399) | 38 (41) | 2.9(4.5) |
| 1977 | 740,000(390,000) | 24(22) | 21,018(17,938) | 21 (25) | 2.8(4.6) |
| 1978 | 950,000(495,000) | 28(27) | 27,040(23,321) | 29 (30) | 2.8(4.7) |
| 1979 | 1,234,000(590,000) | 30(19) | 38,163(32,164) | 41 (38) | 3.1(5.5) |
| 1980 | 1,525,000(730,000) | 23(24) | 54,392(44,437) | 42 (38) | 3.6(6.1) |
| 1982 | 2,057,000(        ) | 16( - ) | 103,295(   -   ) | 38( - ) | 5.0( - ) |

Note:     Figures in parentheses show net sizes.

Source:   Monetary Authority of Singapore, *Annual Reports.*
Morgan Guaranty Trust & Co., *World Financial Markets,* various issues.

wealthy individuals. During the market's initial periods, nonbanking
depositors made up a significant proportion of total deposits (table 6-8).
However, the importance of nonbanking depositors has declined with the entry
of more multinational banks since 1971 and interbank sources have become the
major supplier of funds. Although deposits of the nonbanking sector grew
substantially in size, their proportion of the total liabilities of the ACU fell to 11
to 17 percent. As of the end of 1982, total interbank funds accounted for 77
percent of total liabilities while deposits of nonbanks amounted to 17 percent
of the total. The existence of an active interbank market is a desirable
development for the Asian currency market as it serves the crucial role of
ensuring the allocational efficiency and flexibility of the market.

On the asset side, the relative positions of banking and nonbanking
sources have been just the reverse. Since 1971, loans to nonbanks have
increased substantially both in size and proportion (table 6-8). Commercial
banks and other financial institutions use the market as an additional funding
source to meet temporary needs for domestic liquidity, through the swapping
of Asian currency funds into local currencies. They also use the market to
finance customers directly with loans expressed in U.S. dollars or any hard
currencies. Large regional and national companies, and some smaller ones with
first-class credit standing, are major nonbanking borrowers. Recently,
governments and their agencies have appeared as important users of Asian

currency funds. MNCs, on the other hand, seem to have a preference for local currency financing of their medium-term needs, which minimizes the exchange risk, and their borrowing in the Asian currency market has been mostly short-term, for working capital needs.[14]

Deposit and loan facilities offered in the Asian currency market are similar to those offered in the Eurocurrency market.[15] Most of these deposits and loans are very short-term, the majority having maturities of less than three months (table 6-10). This is because the market has been predominantly an interbank market.

A geographical breakdown of sources and uses of funds in the market shows the maturation of the market as an important regional financial center (table 6-11). The Asian region (including Australia) used to supply about 50 percent of deposits in the market. With an increased flow of funds from the Middle East and the U.S. since 1974, this percentage has fallen. However, the proportion of lending to the Asian region has increased continuously, always exceeding 75 percent of total lending, with borrowers from ASEAN countries, Hong Kong, Taiwan, and Korea who have not been able to finance their hard currency needs via issuing Eurobonds in the Eurobond market. Thus, the Asian region has been a net user of funds, while Europe and the rest of the world have been net sources. This implies that the market has been quite successful as an intermediary, channeling the funds from major capital markets into neighboring developing countries in Asia.

The Singapore government has initiated a number of fiscal and banking incentives and exemptions to boost the market. They include relatively liberal entry policies compared with the domestic market, no reserve and liquidity requirements for ACU banks, no foreign exchange control, the 10 percent concessionary corporate tax rate, and the reduction of stamp duties. These incentives have been instrumental in establishing Singapore as an offshore financial market. However, tax and heavy reporting requirements are often cited as areas where improvements are needed.[16] In contrast to the absence of taxes on offshore loan income in Hong Kong, Singapore charges 10 percent tax on it. M.A.S. reporting requirements are regarded as relatively burdensome compared with Hong Kong. These seem to be responsible for the recent trend that Hong Kong is emerging as a major syndication center, while Singapore remains an interbank funding center. These problems need to be dealt with properly if Singapore is serious about bringing big international borrowers to the market.

So far, important market opportunities of the Singapore banking market have been discussed. In the following, the study will examine how U.S. MNBs have operated in the Singapore market with such opportunities by investigating their motivations for opening branches and their banking activities there.

Table 6-10. Assets and Liabilities of ACUs by Maturities (In million U.S. dollars)

| | Assets | | | | | Liabilities | | | | |
|---|---|---|---|---|---|---|---|---|---|---|
| End of Period | Total | Up to 7 days | Over 7 Days to 3 Months | Over 3 to 12 Months | More Than 1 Year | Total | Up to 7 Days | Over 7 Days to 3 Months | Over 3 to 12 Months | More Than 1 Year |
| 1970 | 384 (100) | 198 (51) | 77 (20) | 106 (28) | 4 (1) | 385 (100) | 30 (8) | 238 (62) | 114 (30) | 2 - |
| 1971 | 1,039 (100) | 165 (16) | 361 (35) | 416 (40) | 98 (9) | 1,049 (100) | 53 (5) | 374 (36) | 596 (57) | 26 (2) |
| 1972 | 2,932 (100) | 374 (13) | 1,072 (37) | 1,234 (42) | 251 (98) | 2,949 (100) | 296 (10) | 1,257 (43) | 1,277 (43) | 119 (4) |
| 1973 | 6,176 (100) | 663 (11) | 2,120 (34) | 3,096 (50) | 298 (5) | 6,192 (100) | 597 (9) | 2,388 (39) | 2,984 (48) | 223 (4) |
| 1974 | 10,157 (100) | 1,032 (10) | 3,795 (38) | 4,597 (45) | 735 (7) | 10,172 (100) | 1,002 (16) | 3,866 (38) | 4,485 (44) | 218 (2) |
| 1975 | 12,402 (100) | 942 (8) | 4,736 (38) | 4,873 (39) | 1,850 (15) | 12,387 (100) | 1,856 (15) | 8,161 (66) | 5,087 (41) | 282 (2) |

## Table 6-10 (continued)

| End of Period | Assets | | | | | Liabilities | | | | |
|---|---|---|---|---|---|---|---|---|---|---|
| | Total | Up to 7 days | Over 7 Days to 3 Months | Over 3 to 12 Months | More Than 1 Year | Total | Up to 7 Days | Over 7 Days to 3 Months | Over 3 to 12 Months | More Than 1 Year |
| 1976 | 17,354 (100) | 2,706 (15) | 8,123 (47) | 3,624 (21) | 2,901 (17) | 17,354 (100) | 4,233 (24) | 9,158 (53) | 3,364 (19) | 599 (3) |
| 1977 | 21,018 (100) | 3,348 (16) | 9,965 (47) | 4,365 (21) | 3,340 (16) | 21,018 (100) | 5,707 (27) | 11,169 (53) | 3,664 (17) | 478 (2) |
| 1978 | 27,040 (100) | 3,862 (15) | 13,079 (48) | 5,550 (21) | 4,548 (17) | 27,040 (100) | 5,957 (22) | 14,619 (54) | 5,622 (21) | 841 (3) |
| 1979 | 38,163 (100) | 5,819 (15) | 17,543 (46) | 7,667 (20) | 7,132 (19) | 38,163 (100) | 8,572 (22) | 20,675 (54) | 7,427 (19) | 1,488 (4) |
| 1980 | 54,392 (100) | 5,918 (14) | 24,366 (45) | 11,747 (22) | 10,361 (19) | 54,392 (100) | 11,839 (22) | 28,666 (53) | 11,127 (20) | 2,769 (5) |
| 1982 | 103,295 (100) | 14,680 (14) | 45,696 (44) | 21,745 (21) | 21,174 (21) | 103,295 (100) | 23,270 (22) | 55,190 (53) | 21,560 (21) | 3,275 (4) |

Note: Figures in parentheses show percentages.

Source: Monetary Authority of Singapore, *Annual Reports*, various issues.

Table 6-11. Geographic Distribution of External Liabilities and Claims of ACU Banks in Foreign Currencies
(In million U.S. dollars)

| Year | Liabilities (Sources of Funds) | | | Total Liability/ Claims | Claims (Uses of Funds) | | | Net Uses of Funds | | |
|---|---|---|---|---|---|---|---|---|---|---|
| | Asia[1] | Europe | All other[2] | | Asia[1] | Europe | All other[2] | Asia[1] | Europe | All other[2] |
| 1971 | 516 (48.5) | 454 (42.7) | 93 (8.8) | 1,063 (100) | 916 (86.2) | 102 (9.6) | 44 (4.2) | 400 | -352 | 49 |
| 1973 | 3,673 (58.5) | 2,083 (33.2) | 521 (8.3) | 6,277 (100) | 4,784 (76.2) | 1,072 (17.1) | 421 (6.7) | 1,111 | -1,011 | -100 |
| 1975 | 6,114 (48.5) | 4,708 (37.4) | 1,775 (14.1) | 12,597 (100) | 10,163 (80.7) | 1,439 (11.4) | 99 (7.9) | 4,049 | -3,269 | -780 |

Note: Figures in parentheses show percentages.
1. Includes Australia
2. Includes the Middle East, the U.S. and Latin America

Source  Monetary Authority of Singapore and its *Quarterly Bulletin*, various issues. Quoted in Hodjera (1978), p. 230.

*U.S. Banking Activities in Singapore*

The U.S. banking presence in Singapore began in 1902 when the First National City Bank of New York (now Citibank) opened its office there. By 1970 Bank of America (1955) and Chase Manhattan Bank (1964) had opened branches there. The activities of these banks in the early days were predominantly trade-related: export and import financing, issuance and notification of letters of credit, foreign exchange transactions, and collection services for traders. Before 1970, the Singapore economy was relatively unsteady and almost entirely dependent upon entrepôt trade. Given the limited and small local economy and the domination of the domestic banking scene by well-established British banks, U.S. banks did not seem to have any significant local business except trade financing.

The notable increase in the U.S. banking presence has actually been made since 1973, when the Singapore government began to issue offshore banking licenses to foreign banks. As of the end of 1980, twenty U.S. banks had branch offices in Singapore, of which four were full license banks and the remaining sixteen were all offshore license banks (table 6-12). In 1983, 25 U.S. banks had branch offices in Singapore. U.S. banks currently hold a dominant position in the Singapore banking scene, though their dominance has declined of late. Two U.S. banks were ranked among the top ten banks in Singapore in 1980, first and fifth respectively. In terms of total assets, the share of U.S. banks among all commercial banks in Singapore was 13.8 percent in 1975 and 23.2 percent in 1980 (table 6-13). Among foreign commercial banks, the share was 16.9 percent in 1975 and 28.1 percent in 1980. In terms of deposits and loans, U.S. banks retained similar market shares. Foreign banks currently hold a market share of more than 80 percent of the overall Singapore banking market, including both onshore and offshore markets. Though no information is available on foreign banks' share in the domestic onshore market, domestic banks seem to dominate the domestic market. Most of the strengths of foreign banks come from their offshore operations, and U.S. banks are no exception to this.

*Major motivations of U.S. banking presence in Singapore.* The eclectic model suggests that the basic factors motivating MNBs to establish a presence in host markets are the desire to exploit maximally their proprietary advantages and specific opportunities in host markets. In this sense, the basic motivation of U.S. MNBs in Singapore is their desire to exploit their proprietary advantages and the market opportunities the Singapore market is providing. The specifics of such advantages and opportunities and their relative importance were examined in chapters 4 and 5 and in the previous sections of this chapter. Here, particular aspects of such market opportunities (location advantages) that complement or facilitate MNB proprietary advantages will be analyzed to find their implications for the patterns of operations of U.S. banks in Singapore,

Table 6-12.  U.S. Banks with Branches in Singapore
(As of the end of 1980)

| Banks | Type of License | Year Commenced Operations | Total Assets in Singapore | Rankings of the Bank in the U.S. (In order of deposits) |
|---|---|---|---|---|
| | | | US $ million | |
| °Citibank | Full License | 1902 | 2,203 | 2 |
| °BOA | " | 1955 | 3,399 | 1 |
| °Chase Manhattan Bank | " | 1964 | 1,861 | 3 |
| °First National Bank of Chicago | " | 1970 | 576 | 9 |
| °Bankers Trust Co. | Offshore License | 1973 | 1,216 | 8 |
| °Continental Illinois | " | " | 572 | 7 |
| °Marine Midland Bank | " | " | 882 | 13 |
| °First National Bank in Dallas | " | " | 176 | 21 |
| °Irving Trust Co | " | 1974 | 514 | 14 |
| °Manufacturers Hanover Trust Co. | " | " | 635 | 4 |
| °Chemical Bank | " | " | 1,285 | 6 |
| °The Bank of New York | " | 1975 | 520 | 18 |

Table 6-12 (continued)

| Banks | Type of License | Year Commenced Operations | Total Assets in Singapore | Rankings of the Bank in the U.S. (In order of deposits) |
|---|---|---|---|---|
| | | | US $ million | |
| °Morgan Guaranty Trust Co. of New York | " | " | 1,320 | 5 |
| °Republic National Bank of Dallas | " | " | 191 | 22 |
| °First Interstate Bank of California | " | " | 236 | 15 |
| °Rainier National Bank | " | 1976 | 148 | 35 |
| °Wells Fargo Bank | " | " | 524 | 11 |
| °Harris Trust and Savings bank | " | 1980 | 394 | 28 |
| °Security Pacific National Bank | " | " | 598 | 10 |
| °First National Bank of Boston | " | " | 474 | 17 |

Note:  1)  All banks have ACU licenses.
       2)  American Express International Co. (AMEX: restricted license
           bank), which is not classified as a  commercial bank for
           reporting purposes in the U.S., is not included.

Source:  Polk's World Bank Directory, various issues.

         A Study of Commercial Banks in Singapore 1980
         (Manila:  The SGV Group).

Table 6-13.  Size and Market Share of U.S. Bank Branches in Singapore
(In million U.S. dollars)

| Year | Total Assets | | | Deposits | | | Loans | | |
|---|---|---|---|---|---|---|---|---|---|
| | Amount | % of all Foreign Banks | % of all banks | Amount | % of all Foreign Banks | % of all banks | Amount | % of all Foreign Banks | % of all Banks |
| 1975 | 7,241 | 16.9 | 13.8 | 5,295 | 19.1 | 16.0 | 1,730 | 14.1 | 11.0 |
| 1978 | 11,644 | 33.0 | 27.3 | 6,815 | 37.5 | 30.9 | 2,399 | 34.3 | 26.2 |
| 1979 | 15,252 | 34.0 | 27.6 | 9,034 | 34.2 | 28.1 | 3,498 | 29.7 | 22.3 |
| 1980 | 17,725 | 28.1 | 23.2 | 10,121 | 27.0 | 22.6 | 3,949 | 24.3 | 18.2 |

Note:  ACU accounts included.

Source:  A Study of Commercial Banks in Singapore 1975, 1978, 1980 (Manila:  The SGV Group).

assuming those banks possess some proprietary advantages for multinational operations.

In chapter 2, several such motivations observable in the process of U.S. bank overseas expansion were explored: (1) to service the financial needs of home country customers operating in foreign countries by way of foreign trade and foreign direct investment; (2) to participate in Eurocurrency offshore markets; (3) to protect market share in the home market; (4) to utilize benefits of "shell" branch status; and (5) to achieve geographic and product diversification. Some of these are particularly noticeable in U.S. MNBs' expansion into the Singapore market.

First, those banks which entered the Singapore market before the opening of the Asian currency market in 1968—Citibank, Bank of America, and Chase Manhattan Bank—can fairly be assumed to be motivated by the desire to service their home customers' foreign financial needs, mostly trade financing and trade-related services. Traditionally, Singapore has been an entrepôt. Before independence, the city had been a major export window for the then-booming tin and rubber industries of the region. The U.S. had active trade with the region for these products, and invested in tin mining and rubber plantations in the region. The three big banks, which already had experience and expertise in international banking, were attracted to the region to serve U.S. traders and investors.

Participation in the offshore banking market as funding sources and lending outlets can be seen as another major motivation for some U.S. banks, especially for those which entered the market during the 1973-74 period. By the time Singapore actively began to pursue policies to establish an offshore financial market in 1973, major U.S. banks already had experience in offshore operations, and began to feel competitive pressures in existing offshore markets. Therefore, the opening of a new market in a region with great potentials easily attracted their attention. Seven major money-center banks (five New York banks and two Chicago banks) and one regional bank (a Dallas bank) opened their branches in the period from 1970 through 1974. These banks had already been operating representative offices in Singapore. The simultaneous entry of competing money-center banks in the new offshore market also suggests the existence of oligopolistic reaction behind their decisions.

The motivations of banks which entered the Singapore market after 1975 are not as clear as those of the earlier groups. However, the defensive motivation and diversification motivation are observable among others. Two New York banks, one Chicago bank, one Dallas bank, and four Pacific coast banks (three California banks and one Seattle bank) have opened their branches since 1975. The U.S. Pacific region traditionally has had active business relations with the Asia Pacific region. As trade and investment volume between the two regions increased, more and more regional customers of Pacific coast banks were involved in the expanding Asia Pacific business. This prompted regional banks to open branches in the Asia Pacific region to serve their customers or to exploit the potential of transregional business. Some opted for Singapore, while others chose other countries in the region as their needs dictated. Those banks which chose Singapore may have considered the emergence of Singapore as a regional offshore market an additional advantage of opening offices there. Along with these motivations, some Pacific coast banks may have seen entry into Singapore as a means of geographic diversification as they faced increasing competitive difficulties in the European market. The opening of Singapore branches by two New York banks during this period was presumably motivated by defensive reasons, along with the banks' independent desire to enter new markets. The leaders, and most of their peers in their home market as well, were already operating in Singapore, and this might have facilitated their decision. Another Dallas-based bank opening an office during this period fits this pattern. Other than this, the pervasive "internationalization boom" among U.S. banks during this period, especially among regional banks, also seemed to have influenced their decisions to enter the Singapore market.

*Major features of U.S. banking activities in Singapore.* The principal activity conducted by U.S. bank branches in Singapore is the acceptance of deposits in the offshore market. Though all U.S. branches are basically permitted to conduct domestic banking operations in Singapore, with different degrees of freedom depending on the status of their licenses, their domestic operations do not seem to be significant compared with their offshore activities, though accurate information is not available. This may be primarily because the domestic market is relatively small, and most U.S. banks are single-office branches (as of the end of 1983, Bank of America had four offices, Citibank and Chase Manhattan Bank each had three, and all others had single offices) with limited resources to capture local business from domestic and foreign banks with extensive local networks. But in the offshore market, U.S. banks do not face such disadvantages. An absence of multiple local branch networks does not constitute a serious disadvantage and U.S. bank branches are not discriminated against in favor of full license and restricted license banks. In offshore operations, the deposit-gathering activity of U.S. MNBs is more significant than the lending activity, which is exceptional compared with other markets in the region.

The Singapore offshore market is generally characterized as a funding source, while Hong Kong serves as a major loan syndication market. This is attributable to the tax rate differentials on offshore loan income between the two markets. MNBs in the Singapore offshore market tend to move their loan booking to their Hong Kong offices to avoid the 10 percent Singapore tax on offshore loan income. This characterization accurately represents U.S. banking operations in both markets. As can be seen from tables 6-14 and 6-15, most U.S. banks use Singapore as a funding source. This implies that U.S. MNBs in Singapore have responded similarly among themselves to the tax rate differentials. The loans/deposits ratio for most U.S. branches is relatively low compared with those of other banking groups. The average loans/deposits ratio of all U.S. banks was 32.7 percent and 39.0 percent in 1975 and 1980 respectively, while the equivalent ratios of all banks, all domestic banks, and all foreign banks were higher. U.S. branches are net suppliers of funds to their head offices and affiliated branches. Only two banks (Bankers Trust Co. and FNB Boston) drew funds from their head offices and related branches to supplement their deposit sources in making loans in Singapore. Regional banks tend more than money-center banks to utilize their Singapore branches as lending outlets of funds generated internally from related offices.

As with the general trends in the Asian currency market, the majority of U.S. banks' deposits come from interbank transactions, though available information does not show a precise proportion. Other important sources of deposits are governments and their agencies, particularly from the Middle East; big regional corporations; multinational corporations operating in the region, mostly from the U.S.; and wealthy individuals, notably the overseas Chinese in the region and the Arabs. Recently, Asian dollar CDs have become an important medium of deposit taking among U.S. banks. In the Singapore offshore market, U.S. banks have been able to afford a slightly more favorable rate for their U.S. dollar deposits than in the U.S., mainly because they have not faced such restrictions as statutory reserve requirements, deposit insurance fees, and interest rate ceilings in the Asian currency market (figure 6-1). This has been instrumental in gathering U.S. dollar deposits in the offshore market.

The extension of credit is another major activity. It involves primarily direct lending to borrowers, and interbank redeposits in the interbank market. In most U.S. bank branches in Singapore, interbank redeposits are slightly greater than direct lending to borrowers.[17] The majority of direct lending goes to big MNCs, creditworthy regional firms, and regional governments and their agencies. Since the middle 1970s, loans to regional governments and government agencies have increased faster than others, as countries in the region have experienced balance of payments deficits and substantial capital needs for their development projects. A substantial part of this lending is done in the form of participation in syndications. Syndication is the most prevalent means of lending when the amount involved is large and the commitment period exceeds twelve months.

Although lending rates in the market vary depending upon borrowers and loan maturities, U.S. banks have usually been able to afford a slightly lower lending rate in the Asian currency market than in the U.S., as Asian currency loans are mostly of large size and of a wholesale nature (figure 6-1).

Table 6-14.  Selected Ratios of U.S. Banks in Singapore

| Banks | Earning Assets /Total Assets 1980 | 1975 | Loans/Deposits 1980 | 1975 | Net Earnings/ Average Earning Assets 1980 | 1975 |
|---|---|---|---|---|---|---|
| All banks | 33.2% | 39.4% | 48.5% | 47.3% | 1.4% | 1.1% |
| All Domestic Banks | 51.7 | 53.7 | 75.7 | 63.1 | 2.2 | 1.2 |
| All Foreign Banks with Full Licenses | 33.8 | 37.5 | 43.6 | 44.1 | 1.7 | 1.2 |
| All Offshore Banks | 25.5 | 32.2 | 40.0 | 44.3 | 0.7 | 0.7 |
| All U.S. Banks | 28.6 | 34.5 | 39.0 | 32.7 | 0.9 | 1.3 |
| B.O.A. | 43.3 | 39.5 | 21.1 | 15.5 | 0.8 | 1.5 |
| Citibank | 22.6 | 17.2 | 38.3 | 22.2 | 1.1 | 2.6 |
| Chase Manhattan | 22.6 | 50.9 | 43.5 | 28.0 | 1.9 | 0.7 |
| FNBC | 13.0 | 30.1 | 41.8 | 51.2 | 0.6 | 2.0 |
| Morgan Guaranty | 16.3 | 51.1 | 24.3 | 51.6 | 0.3 | 0.5 |
| Chemical | 18.7 | 26.2 | 31.4 | 30.4 | 1.0 | 1.6 |
| Bankers Trust | 56.5 | 14.8 | 115.2 | 130.7 | 1.8 | 2.6 |
| Marine Midland | 20.0 | 49.3 | 42.0 | 64.9 | 1.5 | 1.9 |
| Manufacturers Hanover | 35.6 | 17.7 | 56.4 | 26.2 | 1.6 | 1.2 |
| Security Pacific | 2.2 | - | 20.7 | - | 3.6 | - |
| Continental | 38.4 | 97.2 | 43.2 | 98.6 | 0.4 | 0.6 |

Table 6-14 (continued)

| Banks | Earning Assets / Total Assets | | Loans/Deposits | | Net Earnings/ | Average Earning Assets |
|---|---|---|---|---|---|---|
| | 1980 | 1975 | 1980 | 1975 | 1980 | 1975 |
| Wells Fargo | 10.4 | - | 32.0 | - | 0.9 | - |
| New York | 23.7 | 32.1 | 33.1 | 31.5 | (0.1) | 0.1 |
| Irving Trust | 22.9 | 2.2 | 31.7 | 1.8 | 1.4 | (14.6) |
| FNB Boston | 41.5 | - | 135.9 | - | (0.2) | - |
| Harris | 26.1 | - | 26.1 | - | 0.1 | - |
| FIB California | 29.5 | 98.8 | 37.3 | 180.9 | (1.4) | - |
| RNB Dallas | 34.5 | 98.1 | 38.7 | 337.4 | 1.0 | - |
| FNB Dallas | 38.7 | 49.4 | 40.4 | 52.7 | 0.7 | 0.6 |
| Rainier | 21.7 | - | 25.3 | - | 1.0 | - |

Source: A Study of Commercial Banks in Singapore, 1975, 1980 (The SGV Group).

Note: 1) "Earning assets" include maney at call and short notice, loans and advances to customers (including bills receivable), investments in government securities and treasury bills, and other investments.

2) "Loans" include loans and advances to customers (net) and bills receivable.

3) "Deposits" refer to current, fixed, savings, and other deposits of customers, bankers and agents, including negotiable certificates of deposits.

Table 6-15. Claims and Liabilities of U.S. Bank Singapore Branches
to Their Head Offices and Affiliated Branches
(In million Singapore dollars)

| Banks | 1980 | | 1978 | | 1975 | |
|---|---|---|---|---|---|---|
| | Claims | Liabilities | Claims | Liabilities | Claims | Liabilities |
| B.O.A. | 2,120 | 19 | 2,102 | 48 | 1,893 | 87 |
| Citibank | 720 | 4 | 1,340 | 638 | 2,047 | 837 |
| Chase | 0 | 481 | 36 | 978 | 449 | 9 |
| FNBC | 72 | 46 | 83 | 44 | 0 | 205 |
| New York | 0 | 195 | 2 | 3 | 0 | 3 |
| | | | | | | |
| Bankers Trust | 552 | 744 | 505 | 549 | 427 | 99 |
| Chemical | 737 | 3 | 194 | 321 | 0 | 11 |
| Continental | 0 | 25 | 61 | 0 | 7 | 4 |
| | | | | | | |
| FIB | | | | | | |
| California | 90 | 90 | 64 | 0 | 0 | 86 |
| FNB Dallas | 0 | 12 | 0 | 0 | 0 | 24 |
| FNB Boston | 266 | 377 | - | - | - | - |
| Harris | 0 | 5 | - | - | - | - |
| Irving Trust | 23 | 5 | 16 | 0 | 0 | 1 |
| | | | | | | |
| Manufacturers Hanover | 0 | 34 | 508 | 0 | 0 | 50 |

Table 6-15 (continued)

| Banks | 1980 | | 1978 | | 1975 | |
|---|---|---|---|---|---|---|
| | Claims | Liabilities | Claims | Liabilities | Claims | Liabilities |
| Marine Midland | 152 | 95 | 31 | 98 | 4 | 3 |
| Morgan | 707 | 299 | 152 | 354 | 20 | 3 |
| Rainier | 0 | 48 | 0 | 3 | - | - |
| RNB Dallas | 0 | 6 | 0 | 0 | 0 | 168 |
| Security Pacific | 0 | 22 | - | - | - | - |
| Wells Fargo | 0 | 203 | 0 | 269 | - | - |
| Total | 5,439 | 2,713 | 5,094 | 3,305 | 4,847 | 1,590 |

Source: A Study of Commercial Banks in Singapore, 1975, 1978, 1980 (The SGV Group).

Figure 6-1.  Interest Rate Differentials Between the Asian Currency
Market and the U.S.

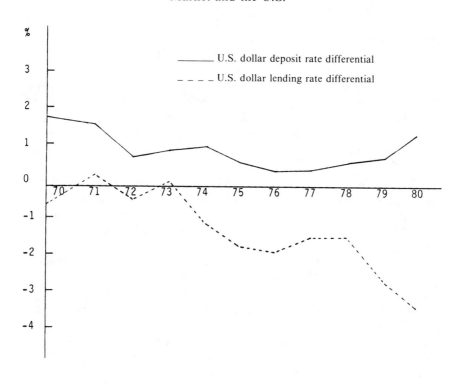

Note:    Deposit rate:
         The Asian currency market: 3-month Eurodollar CD rate
         The U.S. market: 3-month CD rate

         Lending rate:
         The Asian currency market:  Eurodollar prime rate
                                     (3-month CD rate + .05%)

         The U.S. market: U.S. prime rate × 1.2

Source:   Morgan Guaranty Trust Co., *World Financial Markets*, various issues.

Most local deposit taking and lending is done by the three big banks with full licenses and multiple branch networks.[18] However, the importance of local business for these banks is relatively small compared with their offshore business. Though branches with offshore licenses are permitted to conduct local operations in some areas, local business is generally insignificant and sometimes negligible.

Other than these deposit-taking and lending activities, U.S. banks conduct foreign exchange trading, short-term financing of international trade, issuance of guarantees and acceptances, and U.S. dollar clearing services. Foreign exchange trading is becoming an increasingly important operation among U.S. banks. The daily volume of foreign exchange trading in Singapore has grown rapidly from about US$350 million in 1974 to about US$1.8 billion in 1978 and US$2 billion in 1979.[19] Several major U.S. banks have set up or plan to set up regional U.S. dollar clearing centers in their Singapore branches to speed up U.S. dollar clearings for their Asian correspondent banks, and to ease clearing workloads in New York.[20]

Other notable features of U.S. banking operations in Singapore are relatively low profitability and less-than-efficient asset management (table 6-14). These two features are closely related. The below-average earning assets/total assets ratios of most U.S. branches show their poor asset management, and this is directly responsible for their low profitability. This seems to be due primarily to the role of Singapore branches as funding sources for the rest of their MNBs' banking system. However, such judgment needs some reservations, since the calculation of branch profitability involves various allocation problems and tax considerations, and branch asset management is generally dictated by the overall strategic considerations of a bank.

The experience of U.S. MNBs in Singapore shows that they have engaged in similar types of banking activity—offshore deposit taking, offshore lending, interbank transactions and foreign exchange trading, though the levels of involvement in these activities have differed among the banks. Banks with a greater level of ownership advantages, as defined in testing the eclectic model, tend to have higher levels of involvement in such activities. This suggests that location advantages (market opportunities) are more related to the types of activity MNBs perform, while ownership advantages are more related to the levels of their involvement in such activities. This may be primarily due to one major characteristic of the banking industry, the relatively limited scope of product differentiability and innovation. With limited possibilities for product differentiation and innovation in the banking industry, a bank's ownership advantages may be better exploited in reinforcing economies of scale advantages in existing products, rather than in product differentiation and innovation. With limited types of product available and their relatively standardized and known production processes, the selection of the types of product a bank wants to produce may be influenced more by the market opportunities of specific products than by the bank's ability to produce them efficiently, as standardized products generally would not provide much room for efficiency improvement. This would be more pronounced in multinational banking, as MNBs generally have more than necessary levels of ownership advantages for the efficient production of standardized banking products.

*Prospects for U.S. Banking Activities in Singapore*

U.S. banking presence in Singapore has grown remarkably since 1970. In 1970, total assets of U.S. bank branches in Singapore were US$1.2 billion. They grew to US$22.4 billion in 1980, which amounts to an annual growth rate of 29.8 percent. The growth rates of the branches' deposits and loans have been also remarkable at 34.3 percent and 21.6 percent annually, respectively. However, the prospects of U.S. bank branches now would not seem to be as good as they were in the past, as the Singapore market becomes more mature and established. First, one cannot expect to see a continued impressive increase in the numbers of U.S. banks with branches in Singapore in the future. The Singapore domestic banking market is generally regarded as "fully banked" and the offshore banking market has become very competitive with the entry of numerous newcomers and the sluggish international economic situation. Though the emerging potential of ASEAN and of the region in general, and a recovery of the world economic situation may change the market prospects, chances for U.S. banks to expand in the offshore market would not be as great as they were in the past, since most eligible U.S. banks are already operating there, and more aggressive and relatively less-exposed banks from other developed countries and the region are emerging as new powers. Relaxation of U.S. regulations on interstate banking is expected to affect U.S. banks'foreign activities, too, along with future developments of New York's international banking facilities (IBFs) which may divert some activity from overseas offshore markets. Increased opportunities for domestic expansion for major banks may also divert more of their attention toward the U.S. domestic banking market. Therefore, U.S. banks are expected to face relative contractions in terms of their market share in Singapore.

Declining profitability may cause some marginal branches in Singapore to withdraw from the market. Although no banks have withdrawn their branches in Singapore so far, declining profitability may lead to the possibility of their withdrawal as has occurred in other overseas markets. The decline in loan spreads, unfavorable shifts of loan maturities, declining loan management fees, and increased needs for loan reserves have squeezed the profitability of branches. The spreads in the Asian currency market have declined continuously since 1976. During the past few years, the lowest spreads for prime borrowers have declined from 1.25 percent to 1 percent in 1976, to 0.875 percent in 1977, and to 0.5 percent in 1980. At these levels, medium-term lending is regarded as scarcely profitable. The cost of evaluating, reviewing, and administering a credit is variously estimated from 0.25 percent to 0.5 percent per annum, so that current levels provide little for the risk element or for profit. Loan management fees have also declined from 1 percent or more to 0.75 percent or 0.5 percent on a medium-sized loan. Loan maturities have shifted in favor of borrowers toward longer terms. Business undertaken in such conditions may lock in assets of low profitability for long periods. Such market trends may particularly hurt those U.S. banks with no significant cheap funding bases such as customer deposits or internal borrowings from affiliated offices.

In reaction to such market movements and the increasingly sophisticated customer needs, U.S. banks are expected to lead the market in product development and diversification. U.S. banks have already introduced a few new products into the market—the fixed rate U.S. dollar negotiable certificate of deposit (US$NCD), and multinational money management services. Diversification into nontraditional commercial banking activities, such as project financing, investment banking and leasing, will be pursued more actively by U.S. banks to supplement their deteriorating positions in the traditional lending market. Especially, project financing in energy and mining areas is emerging as one of the most promising businesses for U.S. banks in Singapore for the next few years.[21]

Finally, Singapore branches will emerge as regional centers for most U.S. banks in ASEAN countries. With the favorable financial environment in Singapore, prospects for successful consolidation of ASEAN economic cooperation, and the relatively restrictive attitudes of other ASEAN countries toward foreign banks, Singapore branches will be good bases for coordinating or directly executing banking operations within the ASEAN region. This will demand new expertise in branches, different from those of mere deposit-taking and money-lending institutions.

## U.S. Multinational Banking Operations in Korea

*The Commercial Banking Markets in Korea*

With the remarkable economic development since the 1970s, the Korean banking market has experienced unprecedented growth in terms of both quantity and quality. Behind the economic success of the country has been a comprehensive and well-coordinated banking system. In the early stages of the economic development, the banking sector was one of the few sectors of the economy which could support the development process effectively. Banks assumed the role of intermediary, channeling funds to various development projects. The role was unconventional for the commercial banks, considering their traditional function of short-term financial intermediation, but they performed it satisfactorily without creating serious bottlenecks for other sectors. However, the role of intermediary has frequently overshadowed the banks' traditional role of channeling savers' funds to their most effective uses. Now that Korea's economy has grown to the extent that it is not effectively manipulable with central directions, the banking sector has begun to reveal its limitations. It has not been able to meet the economy's new and diverse banking needs efficiently, and currently it is experiencing a restructuring process to provide more efficient services for the new banking demands of the economy.

The Korean banking system consists of two separate groups, the commercial banks and the specialized banks. The first includes the five nationwide banks: The Bank of Seoul and Trust Company, the Commercial Bank of Korea, the Korea First Bank, the Hanil Bank, and the Cho-Heung Bank. In the same group are the ten provincial banks that operate in a particular province and maintain one office in the capital, foreign bank branches and joint-venture banks. There are nine specialized banks concentrating on the provision of capital requirements for the priority sectors, under the direction of the government. They hold about 40 percent of the total assets of the overall banking system. Although they were created for special purposes, some of them, notably the Korea Exchange Bank, the Small and Medium Industry Bank and the Citizens National Bank, conduct most commercial banking activities in direct competition with the commercial banks.

Since 1970, the size of the commercial banking sector increased from total assets of W729 billion in 1970 to W30,015 billion in 1983, an annual average growth rate of 33 percent (table 6-16), not adjusted for inflation. Loans and advances grew by 36 times from W452 billion in 1970 to W16,171 billion in 1983, an annual average rate of 32 percent. During the same time period, deposits of nonbank customers grew by a factor of 29 with time and savings deposits growing by a factor of 23. Capital and reserves grew by a factor of 47. International borrowings of the commercial banks increased by a factor of 109, from W28 billion in 1970 to W3,059 billion in 1983. Acceptances and guarantees, though not a balance sheet item, increased by a factor greater than 49, from W319 billion in 1970 to W15,582 billion in 1983. Most such contingent liabilities were for customers' liabilities to foreign banks. Such remarkable growth of almost all aspects of the commercial banks is quite exceptional by

Table 6-16.    Assets and Liabilities of Commercial Banks in Korea
(In million won)

| | 1970 | 1975 | 1978 | 1980 | 1983 |
|---|---|---|---|---|---|
| Assets | | | | | |
| Cash at hand | 23,227 | 188,363 | 1,094,331 | 1,756,007 | 3,616,400 |
| Amounts due from banks | 162,626 | 1,085,719 | 1,401,655 | 1,549,137 | 2,396,500 |
| Securities | 26,727 | 148,886 | 423,123 | 1,114,983 | 2,563,400 |
| Loans and advances | 451,724 | 2,057,409 | 5,044,182 | 9,332,845 | 16,171,300 |
| Other assets | 64,692 | 373,461 | 1,097,753 | 2,485,126 | 5,267,900 |
| Total Assets | 728,996 | 3,853,838 | 9,062,044 | 16,238,098 | 30,015,500 |
| Liabilities | | | | | |
| Capital and reserves | 33,099 | 224,252 | 378,040 | 781,437 | 1,570,500 |
| Deposits of nonbank customers | 513,615 | 2,213,797 | 5,380,218 | 8,462,454 | 15,045,600 |
| Demand deposits | 123,563 | 562,127 | 1,856,489 | 2,747,091 | 5,542,200 |
| Time and savings deposits | 381,871 | 1,361,173 | 2,984,098 | 5,005,035 | 8,771,900 |
| Other deposits | 8,181 | 290,497 | 539,631 | 710,328 | 731,500 |
| Amounts due to banks | 123,189 | 808,176 | 1,558,126 | 3,064,092 | 7,111,600 |
| Other liabilities | 59,093 | 607,613 | 1,744,660 | 3,930,115 | 6,287,800 |
| Total Liabilities | 728,996 | 3,853,838 | 9,062,044 | 16,238,098 | 30,015,500 |
| (Acceptances and guarantees) | (319,312) | (1,448,426) | (4,565,652) | (10,289,587) | (15,582,400) |

Source:    The Bank of Korea. *Monthly Statistics Bulletin.*

international standards, even though not discounted for inflation. The growth surpassed the country's overall economic growth rate, which was an annual average rate of 29.6 percent in nominal terms during the last decade.

With its expanding size and the strong economy, the Korean banking market has attracted many well-known foreign multinational banks. Although the domestic banking system (both the commercial and the specialized sector) could mobilize domestically a substantial portion of the capital needed for the nation's development projects, it could not meet the needs for foreign capital. To attract foreign capital and promote the internationalization of the nation's economy, the Korean government has actively sought the entry of foreign banks since the middle 1960s. Chase Manhattan Bank was the first foreign bank to open a branch in Korea after World War II, opening its branch in 1967. Ever since then, well-known foreign banks have rapidly entered the Korean market. In 1970, there were six foreign banks. The number increased to nine in 1975 and thirty-nine in 1983, peaking in 1977-78. The rapidly growing economy, prospects for excellent profits, tax advantages, and other privileges attracted many foreign banks during this period.

The size and market share of foreign banks, along with their number, have grown impressively. Total assets of all foreign banks increased 290-fold during the period from 1970 to 1983, from W14.5 billion in 1970 to W4,209 billion in 1983 (table 6-17). This annual average growth rate of 55 percent is more than twice that of the five nationwide commercial banks which are the foreign banks' major competitors in most operations. The foreign banks' market share (in terms of total assets) in the commercial banking sector increased from about 2 percent in 1970 to 14 percent in 1983. Their share in the lending area, which is their main operation, grew from a meager 2 percent in 1970 to 19 percent in 1983. Particularly, their share in foreign currency lending increased from 33 percent in 1970 to 83 percent in 1983. Their profitability (ROI) amounted to 33.1 percent in 1970, 58.9 percent in 1975, 89 percent in 1978 and 64.4 percent in 1983, while the profitability of the five major commercial banks in the same years was 9.3 percent, 50.7 percent, 23.2 percent and 2.0 percent respectively, though different methods of calculating profits and allocation problems make it inappropriate to compare directly the figures for foreign banks and those for

Table 6-17.   Assets and Liabilities of Foreign Banks in Korea
(In million won)

| | 1970 | 1975 | 1978 | 1980 | 1983 |
|---|---|---|---|---|---|
| Assets | | | | | |
| Cash at hand | 86 | 1,035 | 3,504 | 6,153 | 65,000 |
| Amounts due from banks | 2,759 | 66,243 | 59,968 | 138,422 | 182,600 |
| Loans and advances | 9,818 | 131,680 | 685,184 | 1,953,116 | 3,125,500 |
| Call loans | 530 | 2,570 | 7,300 | 10,099 | 127,000 |
| Other assets | 1,327 | 27,528 | 63,563 | 309,119 | 710,000 |
| Total Assets | 14,520 | 229,056 | 819,519 | 2,416,909 | 4,209,600 |
| Liabilities | | | | | |
| Capital and reserves | 1,291 | 8,051 | 32,855 | 82,258 | 132,500 |
| Deposits of nonbank customers | 6,112 | 48,978 | 106,423 | 201,882 | 540,600 |
| Demand deposits | 1,344 | 13,188 | 65,013 | 83,363 | 95,400 |
| Time and savings deposits | 4,196 | 16,384 | 25,683 | 72,467 | 215,300 |
| Other deposits | 572 | 19,404 | 15,727 | 46,052 | 229,900 |
| Interoffice borrowings | 3,743 | 112,034 | 587,973 | 1,875,242 | 3,005,600 |
| Other liabilities | 3,374 | 59,993 | 92,268 | 257,527 | 530,900 |
| Total Liabilities | 14,520 | 229,056 | 819,519 | 2,416,909 | 4,209,600 |
| (Acceptances and guarantees) | (438) | (30,826) | (162,281) | (840,683) | (2,390,000) |

Source:    The Bank of Korea, *Monthly Statistics Bulletin.*

the five commercial banks. Nevertheless, it is generally estimated that foreign banks have enjoyed far higher profitability than domestic banks in Korea.

Such remarkable growth and high profitability have been possible mainly due to the structural peculiarities of the Korean banking sector and the government incentives for foreign banks, along with the foreign banks' superior capabilities for efficient management. Foreign banks have usually been exempted from various government monetary and fiscal policies to which domestic commercial banks have been subject. Examples include exemptions from dealing in low-margin "priority" loans, subscribing to government and monetary stabilization bonds, and maintaining monetary stabilization accounts with the central bank. They are also exempted from income tax and some corporation tax. They suffer from no legal, and few administrative, discriminations compared with domestic banks. Furthermore, higher domestic interest rates have helped them benefit from the full spread between their borrowing costs and lending rates in some foreign currency lendings which constitute about 50 percent to 55 percent of their lending business (figure 6-2). Such freedom and incentives have resulted in a high net profit/capital ratio, despite the two major constraints on their business, to be described below.

First, certain restrictions are imposed on swap transactions, principally with respect to new funds introduced into the country. This is used by the monetary authorities as a flexible technique for regulating the influx of foreign funds. The second restraint is that imposed on the rate of return from local currency lending. Currently, they are allowed a spread of 1 percent above their foreign currency borrowing costs in local currency lending via swap transactions. This prevents them from benefiting from the full spread between their borrowing costs and local lending rates when local lending rates are higher than borrowing costs. However, this restraint turns into a benefit when local lending rates are low. The government pays interest subsidies to foreign banks when domestic lending rates are lower than the banks' borrowing costs in international financial markets, and this actually happened in late 1982.

The conditions leading to profitable operations are expected to continue as the authorities remain determined to retain their relatively liberal attitude towards foreign banks, and the economy continues to need more and more external capital to sustain its growth.

In contrast to the remarkable performance of foreign banks, domestic banks have experienced a relative setback throughout the last decade, and are facing the need for substantial structural transformation. The heart of current problems is the rigidity of the banking system. The rigidity seems to be caused by the absence of interest rates which can equilibrate investment and saving in the economy. This absence has left domestic banks largely in the role of bureaucratic administrators of predetermined government fund allocations. This, in turn, has generated various government monetary and fiscal

Figure 6-2. Interest Rate Differentials Between Korea and the U.S.

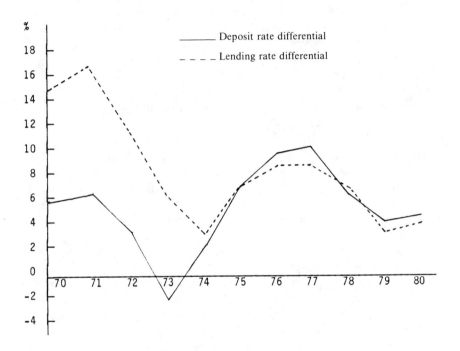

Note:    Deposit rate: 3-month CD rates in each country

         Lending rate:
           Korea: Prime rate
           U.S.: U.S. prime rate × 1.2

Source:  Morgan Guaranty Trust Co., *World Financial Markets,*
         The Bank of Korea, *Monthly Statistics Bulletin,* various issues.

externalities in the banking system. The current banking reform plan is mainly aimed at reducing or eliminating such externalities. However, any reform plans that do not address the basic issue are not expected to lead to the desired results. This seems to be the dilemma the current banking reform plan faces. The government attempts to revitalize the banking sector while at the same time restricting an increase in domestic interest rates to lighten the financial costs of domestic industries.

Besides this basic problem, domestic banks face several operational problems. The most serious one is the large amount of bad loans. Most of these bad loans have been incurred in the area of "priority loans," which often bypass reasonable credit review procedures. The majority of them are said to have become nonearning assets which, however, cannot be easily written off. The size of such assets is estimated by some to be greater than the domestic banks' total capital, and this is one of the causes of domestic banks' low profitability. Another problem is the excessive amount of bank guarantees for their customers' foreign liabilities. Most of these are for large domestic manufacturing firms and construction firms operating in the Middle East. Currently, these guarantees amount to more than ten times the domestic banks' total capital. Such large contingent liabilities seriously hurt domestic banks' capacity to borrow in international financial markets. Unless these problems are dealt with properly, domestic banks will continue to face setbacks relative to foreign banks, which are less exposed and less leveraged.

In sum, it appears that foreign banks, including U.S. MNBs, have sufficient location advantages over local banks in the Korean banking market. Other than various incentives and exemptions allowed by the host government, they do not encounter the operational problems local banks face. This seems to be an exception to a general view that foreign banks tend to have some location disadvantages in the foreign host market against local banks. This has helped the foreign banks to achieve such a remarkable growth in the Korean market compared with local banks, along with superior ownership and internalization advantages in some banking activities.

## U.S. Banking Activities in Korea

The U.S. banking presence in Korea started with the entry of Chase Manhattan Bank in 1967, followed the same year by Bank of America and Citibank. These banks entered the Korean market when the country was launching its first ambitious economic development efforts (the second Five-Year Economic Development Plan) and its economy had just started to have active relations with the world market. The three banks were largely expected to supply much-needed foreign capital and to provide a link with international financial markets. The banks judged that substantial profits would be obtainable from this role and from their other operations in the growing economy. The expectations of both sides were largely proved to be real and justified. The mutual satisfaction attracted more foreign banks into the country.

After remaining cautious for a time, a second group of U.S. banks entered the market in the period from 1977 through 1979. Two Chicago banks and four other major New York banks opened their branches during that period. By this time, the Korean economy had already generated considerable business opportunities for foreign banks, as the market had experienced a continuous shortage of loanable funds. The country's trade, the majority of which was with the U.S. and Japan, had increased tremendously, and there developed sizable business opportunities for these U.S. banks in addition to direct Eurocurrency lendings. In addition, they had a better chance of obtaining government permission to open branches in Korea, as several Korean commercial and specialized banks had opened, or were planning to open, branches in the New York and Chicago areas by that time. Since permission for the operation of foreign banks in Korea has been granted on a basis of reciprocity, U.S. banks from those areas were treated more favorably than those from other areas would have been at that time.

Since 1980, several regional banks, notably from California, have started branch operations in Korea. They have been largely engaged in trade financing and wholesale lending (in both local and foreign currencies) to domestic borrowers. As of the end of 1983, thirteen U.S. banks had branches, and several others were applying for licenses (table 6-18).

Since their initial operations in 1967, U.S. banks have performed impressively. Their total assets grew by a factor of 111 in the last decade, from W11.2 billion (US$36.9 million) in 1970 to W1,247 billion (US$1,889 million) in 1980 (table 6-19). This is equivalent to an average annual growth of 60 percent, which is nearly double that of the five nationwide domestic commercial banks during the same period (an average annual growth rate of 34 percent). The average size of U.S. banks also grew remarkably, from W3.7 billion (US$12.3 million) in 1970 to W42.8 billion (US$88.5 million) in 1975 and to W138.6 billion (US$210 million) in 1980, an average annual growth rate of 33 percent. The U.S. banks' performance in lending and deposit taking is also impressive, though the size of their deposits is far less significant than that of their lending. Total lending increased by a factor of 81 in the last decade, from W8.7 billion (US$28.5 million) in 1970 to W107 billion (US$221 million) in 1975 and to W705 billion (US$1,067 million) in 1980. Foreign currency loans accounted for 60 to 65 percent of this lending. Deposits grew by a factor of about 200 in the last decade, but their size was on the average less than 10 percent of the banks' lending. This shows that U.S. banks in Korea have relied for the majority of their funding on sources other than customer deposits— most notably interoffice borrowings. During the same period, interoffice

Table 6-18.    U.S. Banks[1] with Branches in Korea (As of the end of 1983)

| Banks | Year Commenced Operations | Total Branch Assets[2] (US$ million) | Ranking of the Bank in the U.S. (in order of deposits) |
|---|---|---|---|
| Bank of America | 1967 | 631 | 1 |
| Citibank | 1967 | 602 | 2 |
| Chase Manhattan Bank | 1967 | 479 | 3 |
| FNB of Chicago | 1977 | 59 | 8 |
| Continental Illinois | 1978 | 160 | 7 |
| Chemical Bank | 1979 | 138 | 6 |
| Manufacturers Hanover | 1979 | 229 | 4 |
| Morgan Guaranty | 1979 | 254 | 5 |
| Bankers Trust Co. | 1979 | 62 | 10 |
| Crocker National Bank | 1981 | 67 | 12 |
| Marine Midland Bank | 1981 | 36 | 13 |
| First Interstate Bank of California | 1981 | 46 | 14 |
| Wells Fargo Bank | 1982 | - | 11 |

1. AMEX (1977) is not included.
2. As of the end of 1981.

Source:    The Bank of Korea.
    *Polk's World Bank Directory.*

liabilities increased from W4 billion (US$13.2 million) in 1970 to W987 billion (US$1,495 million), an average annual growth rate of 73 percent. This was faster than the U.S. banks' total asset growth.

Like foreign banks in general, U.S. banks have earned fairly good returns from their investments in Korea. Financial statement data show that U.S. banks' profitability in Korea, measured in terms of return on assets (ROA), has been far greater than that of the five major domestic commercial banks, though slightly less than that of non-U.S. foreign banks, during most of the last decade (table 6-20). It is also higher than their profitability in other markets of the region. However, various limitations in the measurement of bank profitability have made an accurate measurement and a direct comparison among them difficult. Inconsistencies in the allocation of related assets, earnings, and expenses, arbitrary transfer prices, and different accounting practices among banks constitute some of the limitations. Nevertheless, the profitability of foreign banks, including U.S. banks, is believed to be higher than that of domestic commercial banks. In addition to various privileges and incentives given to foreign banks and the effectiveness of their operations, their business practices are often pointed out as a major cause for such higher profitability.

Table 6-19. Size and Market Share of U.S. Bank Branches in Korea (In billion won [million U.S. dollars])

| Year | Total Assets | | | Deposits | | | Loans | | |
|---|---|---|---|---|---|---|---|---|---|
| | Amount | % of All Foreign Banks | % of All Banks | Amount | % of All Foreign Banks | % of All Banks | Amount | % of All Foreign Banks | % of All Banks |
| 1970 | 11.2 (36.9) | 77.4 | 1.5 | 0.4 (1.2) | 6.7 | 0.08 | 8.7 (28.5) | 88.8 | 1.9 |
| 1975 | 128.5 (265.4) | 57.1 | 3.3 | 9.3 (19.3) | 19.0 | 0.4 | 107.1 (221.3) | 81.3 | 5.2 |
| 1978 | 424.4 (876.8) | 51.8 | 4.7 | 28.5 (58.8) | 26.8 | 0.5 | 273.9 (565.8) | 40.0 | 5.4 |
| 1980 | 1,247.0 (1,889.8) | 51.6 | 7.7 | 79.9 (121.1) | 39.6 | 0.9 | 704.6 (1,067.8) | 36.1 | 7.5 |

Source: The Bank of Korea, *Monthly Statistics Bulletin*, various issues.

Table 6-20.    Profitability (Profit/Total Assets) of U.S. Banks in Korea

|  | U.S. banks | Non-U.S. foreign banks | Five nation-wide domestic commercial banks |
|---|---|---|---|
| 1970 | 2.02% | 2.86% | 0.31% |
| 1971 | 2.40 | 3.27 | 0.27 |
| 1972 | 1.15 | 1.18 | 0.76 |
| 1973 | 1.77 | 1.86 | 2.00 |
| 1974 | 2.01 | 2.74 | 2.00 |
| 1975 | 0.87 | 1.85 | 1.86 |
| 1976 | 1.00 | 1.41 | 2.07 |
| 1977 | 0.91 | 1.02 | 0.33 |
| 1978 | 4.14 | -0.53 | 0.73 |
| 1979 | 1.92 | 1.70 | 0.65 |
| 1980 | 2.04 | 2.62 | 0.74 |
| 1981 | 1.29 | 1.03 | 0.40 |

Source:    The Bank of Korea, *Monthly Statistics Bulletin*, various issues.
Euromoney, July 1983.

U.S. banks, along with other foreign banks, generally do not seek retail deposit-taking and lending business, operations with relatively lower margins. They require borrowers to maintain compensatory accounts which are about 10 percent to 15 percent of the loan amounts. By this means they can obtain additional loanable funds at lower costs. The practice has drawn criticisms from customers, since the banks require guarantees of other banks from borrowers when lending and hence have nearly no default risks from their lending. Furthermore, the U.S. banks conduct their operations on a strictly commercial basis, without assuming any of the "policy-related" operations which domestic banks cannot escape.

Such higher profitability of foreign banks often draws comments that various privileges and incentives should be reduced or eliminated. However, no significant movements to change the current liberal policies toward foreign banks are observable in the market.

U.S. banks in Korea, like other foreign banks, largely engage in the lending end of the market. Though the banks provide deposit facilities to customers, most deposits represent either loan-related compensatory accounts or transitory services for customers. U.S. banks do not seem to seek deposits actively for their funding sources, as their limited domestic network and personnel make deposit-taking operations unprofitable. Instead, they concentrate on credit extension—direct loans to customers, call loans in the interbank market, trade financing, and selling acceptances and guarantees.

Two-thirds of U.S. bank loans are foreign currency loans to domestic borrowers, mostly in U.S. dollars, and import financing is an important part of this business. Most syndicated loans are booked in the offices of U.S. banks in offshore financial markets, even though the loans are arranged by the banks' branch offices in Korea. Local currency loans are not as important as foreign currency lending since the branches do not have extensive local deposit bases, and the amounts and spreads of swap transactions for local lending are regulated by the authorities. Most local lending is for the operating capital needs of big domestic borrowers and multinational corporations.

The majority of the U.S. banks' funds for lending come from their invested capital and borrowings from their related offices. With an extensive dollar deposit base in the U.S., and active participation in offshore financial markets, the banks find these among their least expensive and most reliable funding sources. In the last decade, U.S. banks financed about 74 percent of their assets with interoffice borrowings. This clearly shows the use U.S. banks have made of their Korean branches as lending outlets with funds generated in other financial markets and the importance of internal funding facilities for the growth of MNBs. This role coincides with the host country's expectations and seems to be instrumental in getting favorable reception in the host market.

Selling guarantees is another important activity of U.S. banks in Korea. Most domestic banks and firms have not been able to borrow in international financial markets without guarantees of well-known MNBs, due to their limited capital base and lack of international recognition. Even domestic banks with some international reputation have often found it difficult to provide guarantees to domestic borrowers in international financial markets, due to their relatively low capital base. This gives well-known U.S. MNBs good business opportunities with relatively low risks and no actual capital commitment. As U.S. banks usually require guarantees from domestic banks or the government as conditions for issuing guarantees to their customers, they face relatively low or negligible risks in such transactions. Korean MNCs and construction firms operating in the Middle East rely heavily on the guarantee services of U.S. banks. As of the end of 1981, the amount of acceptances and guarantees of U.S. banks in Korea was about 35 percent of the banks' total assets.

In addition to lending and issuing guarantees, U.S. branches engage in foreign exchange trading, interbank lending (call loans), and investment in securities. However, these activities are of limited scale and of noncontinuing nature.

The major difference between U.S. MNBs' activities in Singapore and in Korea comes from the types of activity in which they engage. As hypothesized before, the types of banking activity an MNB conducts in a foreign market appear to be determined by its location advantages in the host market. While deposit taking, foreign exchange trading, and offshore lending constitute major activities of U.S. MNBs in Singapore, these are relatively insignificant activities in Korea. Instead, import financing and local currency lending have been the major activities of U.S. MNBs in Korea. This suggests that the reason that branches of an MNB with the same ownership and internalization advantages operate differently in different markets should be found in the branches' different location advantages in their respective markets.

### Prospects for U.S. Banking Activities in Korea

U.S. banks have shown impressive growth and have remained the dominant power among foreign banks ever since their first presence in the Korean market. However, the relative position of U.S. banks has declined continuously as foreign banks from other countries continue to enter the market. Anticipated market conditions will probably sustain such trends in the near future.

First, U.S. banks will face increased competition from non-U.S. foreign banks, domestic commercial banks, and nonbanking finance institutions of both domestic and foreign origin. The government policy on foreign bank entry suggests that more non-U.S. foreign banks will be allowed to operate in Korea. The need for a diversified portfolio of foreign banks and the principle of reciprocity are the major considerations in permitting foreign banking entry. This tendency will be reinforced by the diversification of external economic relations of the country. Domestic commercial banks, if successfully revitalized by the planned banking reform, will emerge as stronger competitors in the areas of U.S. banks' strength, foreign currency lending and offshore market activities. Nonbanking finance institutions of both domestic and foreign origin, with comparable flexibility and sophistication, which have begun to emerge recently, will form another competitor group in the main areas of U.S. bank operations in Korea. Merchant banks, which are incorporated as joint ventures with major merchant banks and MNBs of Europe and the U.S., have already taken over some of the foreign currency lending business from foreign banks.

Second, various privileges and incentives currently provided to foreign banks are not expected to be continued after a certain period of time. Although one cannot expect any discrimination against foreign banks, the reduction of such benefits will surely affect their market position. Demands for such reduction are heard frequently from domestic banks and other concerned groups.[22] Particularly, the practice of compensatory accounts is a target of criticism.

Third, more Korean firms and banks will participate directly in international financial markets to meet their financial needs. Several firms and domestic banks have already issued bonds and commercial paper or borrowed directly in international financial markets. Though these firms and banks will not switch their business with U.S. banks completely, some portion of lucrative business will be lost.

These are major market movements anticipated in the near future which would affect the operations of foreign banks, particularly U.S. banks, in the Korean market. In response to such market conditions, U.S. banks can plan several strategies to keep their market share and maintain stable growth and profits in the future. Product diversification can be one viable strategy for U.S. banks in this situation. Leasing, project financing, and corporate cash management services are promising areas into which they can diversify. As the financial needs of the market become more sophisticated and comprehensive, demands for these services will increase, as one can observe in more developed markets. These are the areas in which U.S. banks have comparative advantages, as they have already accumulated knowledge and experience in the U.S. and other developed markets. Such fee-based operations require relatively less commitment of financial resources for a given return, and bring relatively higher value-added for a given cost. U.S. banks with a limited domestic funding base and sufficient expertise are the most promising candidates for such operations in the Korean market. Some U.S. banks have already launched these activities, either through expanding existing organizations or establishing separate firms, such as leasing companies or merchant banks.

Expanding the domestic funding base, particularly domestic deposits, can be another strategy for U.S. banks. Generally, this requires extensive branch networks and familiarity with the market, which U.S. banks would often find difficult to achieve. However, difficulties can be partly overcome by specializing in particular geographic areas and depositor groups. Domestic firms with substantial business with foreign countries and foreign MNCs are customers worth approaching. Such tasks will become easier if U.S. banks can provide some additional corporate financial services. Forming joint-venture banks with local partners can be another way to secure sizable domestic deposits. As a domestically incorporated bank, a joint-venture bank would not be discriminated against in establishing multiple branch offices, and local partners can provide necessary market information and knowledge. Furthermore, formation of joint ventures by leading MNBs has been encouraged by the host government. Bank of America recently formed a joint-venture bank.

With secure domestic deposits, U.S. banks can make domestic currency loans without relying on swap transactions, which are regulated in volume and interest spreads. They can also provide a balanced combination of domestic and foreign currency loans, which can solve the inconveniences of customers who currently have to find multiple lenders to finance both domestic and foreign currency needs of the same projects. Furthermore, a stable and extensive domestic deposit base can provide an alternate revenue source when demand for foreign currency loans is low. Such an alternate source is more than justified under the current market trends, in which borrowers tend to switch to weak foreign currency borrowings, such as Japanese yen borrowings, from strong U.S. dollar borrowings.

Other than such strategic considerations, strengthening existing fee-earning operations will, to some extent, bring similar effects. Foreign exchange trading and guarantee-issuing operations seem to be the most promising areas for such purposes. Foreign exchange trading for large commercial and industrial customers and some domestic banks through U.S. banks' extensive networks and their expertise in international foreign exchange markets is an area in which U.S. banks can utilize their existing comparative advantage without committing much additional investment, along with guarantee issuing based on their extensive world-wide capital base.

Such strategic considerations are relevant both for U.S. banks already in Korea and U.S. banks newly entering the market. Particularly, small regional U.S. banks, with limited international networks and U.S. dollar funding sources, are expected to benefit most from such strategies in the Korean market in the future.

**Implications of U.S. MNB Experiences in the Region**

An examination of U.S. MNB activities in the markets of Singapore and Korea shows the importance of certain factors of ownership, location, and internalization advantages over others. Relative importance varies under different market conditions. The size of a bank seems to have a predominant importance in both offshore and onshore markets. Size of branch offices and years of presence in both markets are invariably related to a bank's total size. Generally, the larger a bank, the larger its branch assets and the longer its presence in host markets. The fourteen largest U.S. banks accounted for all thirteen U.S. banks operating in Korea in 1983, (the exception being the ninth-ranked Security Pacific Bank). Among the twenty-five U.S. banks with branch offices in Singapore in 1983 were twenty of the twenty-two largest U.S. banks. Larger banks invariably have superiority in almost all aspects of ownership advantage.

Experiences of U.S. banks also show the fact that location advantages (market opportunities) strongly influence the way an MNB utilizes its proprietary advantages. Particularly, Singapore's relatively favorable market environment for offshore deposit taking and unfavorable pattern of taxation of offshore lending income seem to be largely responsible for U.S. banks' using their branches as funding sources in Singapore and lending outlets in Hong Kong. Favorable environments for lending, especially foreign currency lending, in onshore banking markets direct U.S. MNBs' attention to lending activities in onshore banking markets. The size of host lending markets, interest rate differentials, and unbalanced demands for credits seem to be mainly responsible for such operating patterns.

Thus, it appears that location advantages are more important than other advantages in deciding the patterns of MNB operations, while ownership advantages, particularly bank size, are influential in determining multinational expansion. Branches of the same MNB operate differently in different markets with different location advantages, though they have the same ownership and internalization advantages. Branches of different MNBs in the same market operate quite similarly despite their different ownership and internalization advantages among branches. This seems to suggest that location advantages are more important in deciding an MNB's activities once the MNB reaches a certain level of ownership and internalization advantages, and that the nature of such ownership and internalization advantages are similar among MNBs of the same nationality. This coincides with the conclusions of many studies that ownership advantages are prerequisites of a firm's multinationality.

# 7

# Summary and Conclusions

As one of the few studies on multinational banks, this study has investigated the determinants of the growth of multinational banks and developed an integrated approach to explain the phenomenon of multinationalization in the banking industry. The study has identified various advantages that are essential to the growth of MNBs and the relative importance of these advantages in determining a bank's multinational involvement and the types of banking activity it performs in foreign host markets. The study has also investigated the applicability of various hypotheses and conclusions resulting from prior research on international production and multinational corporations in the manufacturing and extractive industries for international banking and multinational banks and found that the eclectic theory is the most convincing model in explaining the phenomenon of multinational banks.

The eclectic model hypothesizes that a multinational bank is the outcome of a combination of ownership, location, and internalization advantages a bank possesses in a certain foreign market and a certain time period. As defined in the eclectic model, ownership and internalization advantages are bank-specific and location advantages are basically market-specific. Ownership, location, and internalization advantages are dynamic and spread unevenly across markets, banks, and time. Empirical tests supported the hypothesis of the eclectic model and suggested that some advantages were more important than others.

The size of a bank, whether in terms of equity capital, total assets, or total deposits, is the most important ownership advantage in the case of U.S. MNBs. It is invariably related to other ownership advantage factors. Larger banks tend to have a dominant position in almost all aspects of ownership advantage. Larger banks usually have more extensive domestic deposit bases, wider multinational banking networks, and more experience in and more of the technology of multinational banking. They also have well developed and wider intrabank funding facilities. Multinational banking is really a game of size. This reflects a major characteristic of the banking industry. In an industry with relatively limited room for product differentiability and innovation, and relatively standard products, economies of scale tend to dominate among the various advantages necessary for producing certain products. This can explain why multinational banking has been dominated by a number of big banks.

Location advantages are also found to be important for the growth of MNBs. The net effects of location advantages are found to be negative for the growth of MNBs. This is not surprising, considering the fact that the banking industry is basically a regulated industry and the level of such regulation is generally higher for foreign banks than for local banks. Despite various incentives and exemptions in some host markets, the general environments of host markets are not favorable for the growth of MNBs. However, the net effects of location advantages are found to be favorable for the profitability of MNBs. This seems to imply that host governments are more concerned with preventing foreign dominance of local banking markets than with limiting the earnings of foreign banks. The finding coincides with the general policy direction of host governments in dealing with foreign banks, which centers on preserving the independence of monetary policies within their countries. However, any conclusion with regard to profitability should be made tentatively due to the possible arbitrariness of the profit performance shown in the books of foreign branches.

The effects of individual location advantage factors are found to differ across banking activities and markets. In the onshore banking markets, the lending rate differential, foreign exchange rate changes, and the size of a host banking market are instrumental for the growth of total assets of U.S. MNB branches, while only the lending rate differential is significantly related to the growth of U.S. MNB branch lending. Both foreign exchange rate changes and the size of a host banking market are important for the growth of deposits accepted in foreign branches of U.S. MNBs. The relatively insignificant role of the deposit rate differential for the growth of foreign branch deposits appears to be due to the nature of those deposits in the onshore market—mostly loan-related compensatory deposits and transitory deposits, which are relatively insensitive to deposit rate changes. The size of a host banking market is found to be highly correlated with the degree of home country business involvement in the host market.

In the offshore markets, no individual location advantages are found to be significantly related to the growth of U.S. MNB branches. This implies that the host offshore market (Singapore) has not provided U.S. MNBs with any significantly favorable location advantages compared to the U.S market.

The tests produce inconclusive results with regard to the relationship between individual location advantages and branch profitability in both markets. The possibility of arbitrary realization (or removal) of profits in (or from) the books of MNB branches during the test periods may be one explanation for the results.

The availability and ease of internal transactions are another important determinant of MNB growth. Transactions via internal channels can reduce transaction costs unavoidable in external markets. This is more pronounced in information transactions, which are a major feature of multinational banking and the banking industry in general. The existence of extensive and efficient internal markets enables MNBs to scan worldwide business opportunities and to move funds quickly for their most efficient use.

The study has also found that location advantages are largely responsible for the types of banking activity an MNB performs in a foreign market and that ownership and internalization advantages are more relevant in deciding the level of involvement in certain banking activities. This results primarily from that banking industry's characteristics discussed before—relatively limited scope of product differentiability and innovation, and relatively standardized products with simple production processes.

Finally, the study findings suggest that Dunning's eclectic approach is expandable to a service industry and provides a general model from which the emergence of different modes of multinational business involvement can be explained and predicted as special cases.

The findings in this study present a number of implications for the banking industry and the host governments. The findings provide an MNB with a more systematic way of evaluating its current banking activities or selecting new banking activities it wishes to perform in a foreign market. The evaluation and selection are generally done on the basis of prospects for short-term profitability and contribution to the profitabilities of other activities. The evaluation and selection process often involves unsystematic assumptions and arbitrary allocations. Decisions are often made without considering which activities can utilize the bank's resources and market opportunities most efficiently. The findings of this study can amend such weaknesses of current evaluation practices. The findings suggest a way to find what kinds of advantage (or prospects for advantage) are important for the growth of a given banking activity and to enable the MNB to find the kinds of banking activity in which it can best utilize its current (or prospective) advantages and market opportunities. This can be a good supplement to the current evaluation practices, bringing them a more strategic perspective.

For the host governments, the study can suggest the types of location advantage they should provide to attract MNBs to conduct certain desired banking activities in their countries. For instance, the host governments can induce MNBs to supply them with more foreign capital by offering tax incentives for the interest income from their foreign currency lending or maintaining a favorable interest rate structure for foreign currency lending when they need an increased influx of external capital. Furthermore, the findings suggest to host governments a simple way of selecting MNBs they want to invite. As the size of a bank is found to be MNBs' most important ownership advantage and closely related to other ownership advantages, host governments can reduce their review and evaluation work by limiting the minimum size of applicant foreign banks; they need not review and evaluate the various ownership advantages of individual applicant banks. In this respect, the practice in some countries of requiring applicant foreign banks to be within a certain range in their rankings in the home and world markets seems to be reasonable and well-intentioned. However, the practice may not necessarily be reasonable in terms of economic welfare as it might encourage the monopolization or oligopolization of multinational banking by a number of big MNBs.

This study has centered on the foreign branch activities of multinational banks. There is, however, another important form of multinational banking involvement, the foreign banking subsidiary (wholly or partially owned), with which this study has not dealt. The motivations of MNBs to form foreign banking subsidiaries are believed to be different from their rationale for establishing foreign branches, and the activities of foreign banking subsidiaries appear to be different from the activities of foreign branches.

Though this study did not include MNBs' foreign subsidiary activities due to possible problems of inconsistency and incomparability, a subsidiary form is often found to be the only means by which an MNB can serve certain foreign markets. Moreover, a subsidiary form is often preferred to other organizational forms in serving particular foreign markets. Its importance in multinational banking deserves further study. Furthermore, a comparative study of the branch and subsidiary forms of multinational banking involvement will provide a better understanding of MNBs.

In addition, this study has focused on U.S. MNBs. Though U.S. MNBs have been the most dominant group in multinational banking, MNBs from other countries have become increasingly noticeable in the multinational banking scene. Non-U.S. MNBs have different ownership, location, and internalization advantages. A comparative study will uncover different patterns of multinational involvement of banks of different nationalities and identify the effects of several location advantage factors that this study could not test, such as tax differentials, nationality of a bank, and competitive situations of the home banking market.

Finally, the multinationalization phenomenon of other service industries, such as the hotel industry, the insurance industry, the advertising industry, and the accounting service industry can be explored by the eclectic approach which proved to be satisfactory in explaining the multinationalization of the banking industry. This will help expand the scope of international business studies and explain the different patterns of multinationalization of various industries.

# Appendix A

# Correlation of Variables
# (Cross-Section Analysis)

**1975**

|        | IVO$_1$ | IVO$_2$ | IVO$_3$ | IVO$_4$ | IVL M  | IVI$_1$ | IVI$_2$ |
|--------|---------|---------|---------|---------|--------|---------|---------|
| IVO1   | 1.0000  |         |         |         |        |         |         |
| IVO2   | 0.8283  | 1.0000  |         |         |        |         |         |
| IVO3   | 0.9443  | 0.7083  | 1.0000  |         |        |         |         |
| IVO4   | 0.9592  | 0.8492  | 0.8278  | 1.0000  |        |         |         |
| IVL M  | 0.5720  | 0.5233  | 0.5646  | 0.5371  | 1.0000 |         |         |
| IVI1   | 0.5722  | 0.4959  | 0.5680  | 0.5366  | 0.9966 | 1.0000  |         |
| IVI2   | 0.8746  | 0.6268  | 0.9153  | 0.7406  | 0.4745 | 0.4788  | 1.0000  |

**1978**

|        | IVO$_1$ | IVO$_2$ | IVO$_3$ | IVO$_4$ | IVL M  | IVI$_1$ | IVI$_2$ |
|--------|---------|---------|---------|---------|--------|---------|---------|
| IVO1   | 1.0000  |         |         |         |        |         |         |
| IVO2   | 0.8421  | 1.0000  |         |         |        |         |         |
| IVO3   | 0.9429  | 0.6514  | 1.0000  |         |        |         |         |
| IVO4   | 0.8974  | 0.7666  | 0.8251  | 1.0000  |        |         |         |
| IVL M  | 0.4144  | 0.3324  | 0.4104  | 0.3702  | 1.0000 |         |         |
| IVI1   | 0.4114  | 0.3290  | 0.4164  | 0.3699  | 0.9930 | 1.0000  |         |
| IVI2   | 0.9004  | 0.6819  | 0.8878  | 0.9127  | 0.3354 | 0.3394  | 1.0000  |

**1980**

|        | IVO$_1$ | IVO$_2$ | IVO$_3$ | IVO$_4$ | IVL M  | IVI$_1$ | IVI$_2$ |
|--------|---------|---------|---------|---------|--------|---------|---------|
| IVO1   | 1.0000  |         |         |         |        |         |         |
| IVO2   | 0.8162  | 1.0000  |         |         |        |         |         |
| IVO3   | 0.9283  | 0.6041  | 1.0000  |         |        |         |         |
| IVO4   | 0.9162  | 0.7687  | 0.8122  | 1.0000  |        |         |         |
| IVL M  | 0.3427  | 0.2942  | 0.2647  | 0.4057  | 1.0000 |         |         |
| IVI1   | 0.3227  | 0.2713  | 0.2537  | 0.3724  | 0.8931 | 1.0000  |         |
| IVI2   | 0.8681  | 0.6289  | 0.8518  | 0.8774  | 0.3610 | 0.3431  | 1.0000  |

# Appendix B

## Correlation of Variables (Pooled Time Series Cross-Section Analysis)

*Korea (1973-1980)*

| | IVO₁ | IVO₂ | IVO₃ | IVO₄ | IVL₁D | IVL₁L | IVL₂ | IVL₃ | IVL₄ | IVL₅ | IVI₁ | IVI₂ | IVL₇ |
|---|---|---|---|---|---|---|---|---|---|---|---|---|---|
| IVO1 | 1.0000 | | | | | | | | | | | | |
| IVO2 | 0.6729 | 1.0000 | | | | | | | | | | | |
| IVO3 | 0.9387 | 0.4418 | 1.0000 | | | | | | | | | | |
| IVO4 | 0.1599 | -0.0719 | 0.1769 | 1.0000 | | | | | | | | | |
| IVL1D | 0.0581 | -0.0457 | 0.0666 | 0.2712 | 1.0000 | | | | | | | | |
| IVL1L | 0.3144 | 0.2013 | 0.2699 | -0.1750 | 0.5831 | 1.0000 | | | | | | | |
| IVL2 | -0.1706 | -0.1341 | -0.1413 | 0.2371 | -0.1154 | -0.3784 | 1.0000 | | | | | | |
| IVL3 | -0.2176 | -0.2948 | -0.1829 | 0.4811 | 0.5928 | 0.0605 | -0.4467 | 1.0000 | | | | | |
| IVL4 | 0.2169 | 0.3083 | 0.2055 | -0.4393 | -0.2991 | -0.1791 | 0.5153 | -0.8193 | 1.0000 | | | | |
| IVL5 | 0.4098 | 0.4772 | 0.3482 | -0.6918 | -0.3273 | 0.2132 | -0.0772 | -0.7744 | 0.7066 | 1.0000 | | | |
| IVI1 | -0.2204 | -0.3773 | -0.2139 | 0.4492 | 0.1660 | -0.2519 | 0.1247 | 0.4683 | -0.4131 | -0.6206 | 1.0000 | | |
| IVI2 | 0.8102 | 0.3053 | 0.8908 | 0.3029 | 0.1304 | 0.2587 | -0.1507 | -0.0397 | 0.0492 | 0.1751 | -0.1373 | 1.000 | |
| IVL7 | 0.1168 | 0.0748 | 0.1105 | -0.2271 | -0.1651 | 0.3115 | -0.6671 | 0.1369 | 0.2932 | -0.0162 | -0.1492 | 0.1276 | 1.0000 |

*Singapore (1975, 1978, 1980)*

| | IVO₁ | IVO₂ | IVO₃ | IVO₄ | IVL₁D | IVL₁L | IVL₃ | IVL₄ | IVL₅ | IVI₁ | IVI₂ |
|---|---|---|---|---|---|---|---|---|---|---|---|
| IVO1 | 1.0000 | | | | | | | | | | |
| IVO2 | 0.8482 | 1.0000 | | | | | | | | | |
| IVO3 | 0.9243 | 0.6679 | 1.0000 | | | | | | | | |
| IVO4 | 0.7312 | 0.5965 | 0.6800 | 1.0000 | | | | | | | |
| IVL1D | -0.0649 | -0.0922 | 0.0080 | 0.2707 | 1.0000 | | | | | | |
| IVL1L | 0.0606 | 0.0857 | -0.0073 | -0.2465 | -0.9960 | 1.0000 | | | | | |
| IVL3 | -0.0629 | -0.0940 | 0.0098 | 0.3304 | 0.3100 | -0.2241 | 1.0000 | | | | |
| IVL4 | -0.0788 | -0.1145 | 0.0108 | 0.3656 | 0.8566 | -0.8073 | 0.7561 | 1.0000 | | | |
| IVL5 | 0.0739 | 0.1090 | -0.0108 | -0.3671 | -0.5677 | 0.4921 | -0.9587 | -0.9111 | 1.0000 | | |
| IVI1 | -0.0023 | -0.0133 | 0.0655 | 0.2447 | 0.6322 | -0.6288 | 0.2064 | 0.5472 | -0.3679 | 1.0000 | |
| IVI2 | 0.8641 | 0.6696 | 0.8459 | 0.7309 | -0.0614 | 0.0629 | -0.0005 | 0.0425 | 0.0188 | 0.0553 | 1.0000 |

# Notes

**Chapter 2**

1. See Porzecanski (1981), p. 9:

   > In 1976, the profit margin on domestic assets of the ten internationally most active American Banks averaged 0.40% while the return on international assets was 0.52%. Since that time, however, falling spreads on loans to virtually all foreign borrowers have helped to reverse the banks' profit picture, with return on international assets dropping gradually to 0.44% in 1979.... Consequently, the contribution of international earnings to total bank earnings has tended to decline from a record high of 50% in 1975 to a low of 43% in 1979.

2. Rockefeller (1964), p. 75.

3. Lees (1974), pp. 66-67.

4. Henning, Pigott and Scott (1978), p. 193.

5. As of October 1978, U.S. agencies of foreign banks had an outstanding balance of $11,457 million of borrowings from commercial banks in the U.S. while their liabilities to directly related institutions amounted to $15,212 million. (Source: Board of Governors of Federal Reserve System, data released in March 1979. Quoted in Khoury, 1980, pp. 92-93.)

6. In some cases, a subsidiary is allowed to engage in some banking activities which are not permitted to domestic banks. In the U.S., a subsidiary of a foreign bank can engage in brokerage and underwriting businesses which are forbidden to U.S. domestic banks.

7. Mexico and Canada are good examples of this case. Even within the U.S., banking regulations in California require foreign banks soliciting deposits to be organized as subsidiaries.

8. See Reed, Cotter, Gill and Smith (1976), p. 368 and Frowen (1979), p. 14.

9. Frowen (1979), p. 145.

10. One of the most recent cases is the borrowing plan proposed by the Korea Development Bank. The bank actually asked several prime MNBs to participate in the loan packages under specific terms it formulated.

11. Dufey and Giddy (1978), p. 223.

12. Ibid., p. 226.

13. Davis (1980), p. 96.

14. Hanley (1976), p. 38.

15. The most dramatic example in recent years is the collapse of Herstatt Bank in mid-1974 due to the bank's careless engagement in foreign exchange operations.

16. Davis (1980), p. 89.

17. The following comments reflect well the sentiment among MNBs a decade ago:

    > It all seemed so obvious a decade ago. Any bank that wanted to be considered a major institution had to be an international bank, with branches dotted around the world—a bank with "global reach," as the bankers liked to say. And anyone who doubted this was simply a fool or a narrow-minded chauvinist. According to one story that made the rounds of international bankers, an executive at one major American institution who had the temerity to question whether his bank's worldwide expansion was really such a good idea was promptly banished to Australia for raising such a silly idea. This executive, so the story goes, spent the rest of his career in the outback contemplating the error of his ways.

    Neil Osborn, "The Profit Squeeze Comes to International Banking," *Institutional Investor*, June 1981, p. 239.

18. Osborn (1981), p. 241.

19. Annual reports (1978, 1979, 1980) of Chase Manhattan Bank and Osborn (1981), p. 241.

20. The Bank of America division that includes the bank's European offices turned in a return on assets of 0.46 percent in 1980, which was worse than almost any other BOA units. Chase Manhattan Bank achieved a mere 0.22 percent return on assets in Europe in 1980, compared with 0.53 percent for the bank as a whole. The same is true in the case of several major European banks in the U.S. In Japan, ROA for all foreign banks has declined from 1.12 percent in 1975 to 0.33 percent in 1979.

21. In March 1981, France's Caisse Nationale des Télécommunications arranged a ten-year standby credit with 0.25 percent-over-LIBOR element in the spread. To this, says Patrick Haizet, general secretary of Banque Française du Commerce Extérieur, "[such a lending] must generate 1.25 margin to make the whole thing profitable if you include all your costs and at least some risk." Osborn (1981), p. 245.

22. For two Singapore banks and Hong Kong & Shanghai Banking Corp., see Osborn (1981), p. 242.

23. Citibank chairman Walter Wriston used to say, "Countries don't go bankrupt."

24. This point is shown in Moore (1963), p. 3.

25. Robinson (1972), p. 15.

26. See Brimmer (1975, pp. 12-24), Robinson (1972), Brimmer and Dahl (1975, pp. 341-63), Goldberg and Saunders (1980, pp. 630-43), Baker (1978, p. 6), Khoury (1980, pp. 51-76), and Kelly (1977, pp. 83-108).

27. Khoury (1980), pp. 152-53.

28. Periodical classification is largely borrowed from the classification used in Robinson (1972), but is by no means definitive.

29. See Kouzoul (1970).

30. Tamaga and Willis (1956), pp. 1290-92.

31. They were First National City Bank of New York, First National Bank of Boston, Bank of America, N,T. & S.A., Chase Manhattan Bank, Bankers Trust Company, Guaranty Trust Company, and Hanover Bank. All six except First National Bank of Boston had their branches in Europe and other areas, while FNBB had no branches in Europe—it had several in Latin America. All seven banks set up their foreign branches before 1945.

32. Robinson (1972), pp. 197-98.

33. Knickerbocker (1973).

34. In early 1969, the Federal Reserve Board began to approve the creation of "shell" branches in offshore money markets (especially Nassau and the Cayman Islands).

35. Khoury (1980), p. 68.

36. Brimmer and Dahl (1975), p. 346.

37. Brimmer (1975), pp. 12-16.

38. The rationale behind the Federal Reserve Board's approval of the creation of shell branches was to provide smaller banks, which could not justify the high overhead expense of overseas branch operations in such locations as London or Frankfurt, with a means of obtaining access to the Eurodollar market.

39. Brimmer and Dahl (1975), p. 347.

40. Johnston (1977), p. 37.

41. Porzecanski (1981), p. 10 and individual banks' annual reports.

42. "The New Banking," *Business Week*, September 15, 1973, p. 70. A senior vice-president of one of the largest U.S. banks pointed out, "We have one major product: great big loans to great big companies. If anything happens, our profits are vulnerable."

**Chapter 3**

1. Here the licensing agreement includes technical know-how licensing, management contracting, and franchise agreement.

2. Aliber (1976), p. 5.

3.  Ibid., p. 6.

4.  "A 1975 *Fortune* magazine showed that 82 percent of the top 500 companies had changed their banking relationships in the previous nine years, most commonly in order to increase their access to funds or to get better international services in more locations." G.R. Thoman, "How to Serve the MNC Market," *The Banker,* August 1977.

5.  They were, typically: (1) the Interest Equalization Tax Act (1964) designed to curb foreigners' access to United States capital markets; (2) the Voluntary Foreign Credit Restraint Program (1965) designed to curtail the foreign lending of United States commercial banks; and (3) the Overseas Foreign Direct Investment Guidelines designed to limit American corporations' ability to transfer funds overseas for direct investment.

6.  Rugman (1981), chapter 5.

7.  Coase (1937), p. 390-93. He identifies the four types of costs of using a market: the brokerage cost of finding a correct price; the cost of defining the obligations of parties in a contract; the risk of scheduling and related input costs; and the taxes paid on exchange transactions in a market.

8.  Rugman (1981), p. 92.

9.  Rugman (1980).

**Chapter 4**

1.  Dufey and Giddy (1981, p. 34) view the attributes as promised yield, expected rate of return, rate of return risk, liquidity or marketability, maturity or duration, assurance of availability of funds or claims, divisibility, currency of denomination, and country of jurisdiction.

2.  Citicorp and White, Weld & Co. were the institutions that introduced the Eurodollar certificates of deposit (Euro CD or London dollar CD). They spent fifteen months in tortuous discussions and legal inquiries; yet the first buyer of a $25,000 London CD was Chemical Bank in London, which promptly began printing its own in blatant imitation. See Von Clemm (1976), p. 608. Quoted in Dufey and Giddy (1981), p. 40.

3.  Dufey and Giddy (1981) view most financial innovations, except those designed to circumvent regulations, as no more than a change in the combination of features of existing instruments.

4.  The significance of the ownership-specific advantages derived from nationality and brand names of banks in international banking is discussed in Giddy (1981).

5.  See Stoll (1968), Branson (1969), Prachowny (1970), and Officer and Willett (1970) for the causes of the existence of unexploited profit opportunity for arbitrage in the foreign exchange market.

6.  Buckley and Casson (1976). Imperfect markets for knowledge are the basis of their theory of the multinational enterprise.

7.  Casson (1979).

8.  Gray and Gray (1981), pp. 42-44.

9.   Ibid., p. 42.

10.  Yannopoulos (1973).

11.  Kindleberger (1974). Simultaneous communication over many time zones is sometimes impossible and, at least, dislocates the working day for at least one partner.

12.  Giddy (1981). Giddy tested this advantage by regressing the foreign exchange profits of U.S. banks on the number of foreign countries in which each bank has offices. He found a statistically significant positive relation between them.

13.  Fieleke (1977). Fieleke tested this hypothesis by regressing the variance of the percentage rate of return on net worth on average assets and international earnings (as a percent of total earnings) of the thirteen U.S. banks for the period from 1970 to 1976. The result was not conclusive, but he did not rule out possibilities of influences of other factors such as differences in portfolio composition from bank to bank.

14.  Dunning (1979), pp. 275-76.

15.  Little (1969), p. 6. "Although this margin may vary over time, . . . this figure is a good estimate of the margin applied to loans to prime borrowers."

16.  Little (1969), p. 6; Dufey and Giddy (1978), p. 53.

17.  Host countries in the region generally do not engage in the American practice of requiring that a certain percentage of a loan be kept as a demand deposit with the lending bank. However, some U.S. banks impose this practice in some onshore markets.

18.  Aliber (1976), p. 6. In addition, banks that face various obstacles in expanding domestically, which is a typical characteristic of oligopolistic markets, usually seek opportunities to expand in foreign markets.

19.  Here, offshore banking markets refer to London, Brussels, Luxembourg, Zurich, Beirut, Bahrain, Singapore, Hong Kong, the Bahamas, the Cayman Islands, Panama City, and the Netherlands Antilles.

## Chapter 5

1.   The size of a bank's equity capital determines the amount of lending the bank can provide under current banking regulations on lending. The prospects of lending, in turn, ultimately determine the overall size of deposits to be accepted.

2.   The importance of these three aspects of consideration in determining the relative importance of variables is well explained by Gordon (1968) and Johnston (1963).

3.   See Brimmer and Dahl (1975), Fieleke (1977), and Goldberg and Saunders (1980, 1981).

## Chapter 6

1.   Western bankers, particularly the Americans, believe that the Japanese banks have led this rate-cutting practice in Eurocurrency lendings to the region. See *Far Eastern Economic Review* (March 2, 1979), pp. 91-92.

2. Dufey (1981), p. 28.

3. In the 1960s, Indonesia rescheduled her external debts four times: in 1966, 1967, 1968, and 1969. See Bee (1977), pp. 33-36.

4. See table 2-9.

5. U.S. regulations on capital outflow of the late sixties and early seventies could have affected multinational expansions of U.S. banks both positively and negatively. On the one hand, the regulations might have encouraged U.S. banks' multinational expansion to serve their multinational customers which could not move capital from their U.S. parents freely. On the other hand, the regulations might have discouraged the opening of overseas branches of U.S. banks, particularly in the regions which were net borrowers of funds rather than funding sources, as U.S. parent banks could not supply necessary capital for their overseas branch operations. Though the net effects of these regulations on overseas banking expansion have not been clearly identified, the fact that U.S. multinational banking expansion has tremendously increased in most regions of the world since the removal of these regulations seems to suggest, at least, the possibility of minimal positive effects on U.S. banks' multinational expansion.

6. Initially, offshore license banks could only grant medium- and long-term loans to residents, which were of a minimum of S$1 million and of two years or more.

7. Wong (1975), pp. 101-2.

8. Tan (1981), p. 19.

9. Liquid assets include cash, balances with M.A.S., money at call with discount houses, Treasury bills, trade bills, and S$NCD. See Lee and Jao (1982), footnote 9 on p. 311.

10. Lee (1974), pp. 115-18 and table 6-9.

11. Monetary Authority of Singapore (1980), p. 96.

12. The Banking Act stipulates the minimum capital requirements of banks (currently, domestic banks: S$3 million, foreign banks: S$6 million), the minimum reserve requirements (currently 6 percent of all the relevant deposits), the minimum liquidity ratio (currently, 20 percent of the bank's liabilities base), the limit for certain types of banking activities, and the prohibited transactions.

13. Hodjera (1978), p. 222.

14. Bhattacharya (1977), p. 37.

15. Deposits accepted are (a) sight; (b) two-day to seven-day notice; and (c) fixed-term maturities of up to five years. Loan facilities offered are (a) short-term, including overnight; (b) fixed-interest rate loans for various maturities that often exceed one year; (c) lines of credit for commercial transactions, for a fixed term but subject to a rollover; and (d) floating interest rate credits exceeding one year on which the interest rate, based on the interbank offer rate plus a margin, is adjusted every three to six months.

16. *Far Eastern Economy Review* (February 10, 1978), p. 76. *Far Eastern Economy Review* (April 4, 1980), p. 78.

17. As of the end of 1980, the share of interbank redeposits of overall U.S. bank branches in Singapore was roughly 54 percent of their total direct credit extensions (interbank redeposits: S$8,941 million, loans and advances to nonbank customers: S$7,643 million). In 1975 and 1978, the share was 46 percent and 49 percent respectively. BOA shows the share as high as 70 percent in 1980. (Source: *A Study of Commercial Banks in Singapore*, 1975, 1978 and 1980, The SGV Group).

18. The proportion of local deposits and lendings of these banks and others are not available in publicized data. However, several sources including some of these banks implied the proportion was mostly insignificant.

19. *Far Eastern Economic Review*, April 4, 1980, p. 78. The currency composition of foreign exchange trading in Singapore is approximately US$–yen trade 31 percent, US$–deutschemarks 24 percent, US$–sterling 20 percent, other combinations of third currencies 12 percent, and Singapore dollar–foreign currencies 13 percent.

20. LaPorte and Young (1981), pp. 149-53.

21. "Singapore is attracting energy experts as banks gear up for oil and gas loans," *The Wall Street Journal*, February 5, 1982, p. 30.

22. For example, see *Mae-il Kyongje Shinmoon (Daily Economic News)* No. 4819, August 11, 1982.

# Bibliography

Aliber, R. "Toward a Theory of International Banking," *Economic Review*, Federal Reserve Bank of San Francisco (Spring 1976), pp. 5-8.

Allen, D. and Giddy, I. "Towards a Theory of Interdependence in Global Banking Regulation," *Eastern Economic Journal* (December 1979), pp. 445-52.

Baker, J. *International Banking Regulation*. New York: Praeger Publishers, 1978.

Bee, R. "Lessons from Debt Reschedulings in the Past," *Euromoney* (April 1977), pp. 33-36.

Bhattacharya, A. *The Asian Dollar Market: International Offshore Financing*. New York: Praeger Publishers, 1977.

Branson, W. "The Minimum Covered Interest Differential Needed for International Arbitrage Activity," *Journal of Political Economy*, vol. 77, no. 6 (1969), pp. 1028-35.

Brimmer, A. "Perspectives on Foreign Activities of American Banks," *Testimony before the Subcommittee on Financial Institutions, Supervisions, Regulation and Insurance of the Committee on Banking, Currency and Housing, U.S. House of Representatives*, December 5, 1975.

Brimmer, A. and Dahl, F. "Growth of American International Banking: Implications for Public Policy," *Journal of Finance*, 30 (May 1975), pp. 341-63

Buckley, P. and Casson, M. *The Future of Multinational Enterprise*. New York: Holmes & Meier, 1976.

Casson, M. *Alternatives to the Multinational Enterprise*. London: MacMillan, 1979.

Caves, R. "International Corporations: The Industrial Economics of Foreign Investment," *Economica* (February 1971).

Coase, R. "The Nature of the Firm," *Economica*, 4 (November 1937), pp. 386-405.

Davis, S. *The Eurobank: Its Origins, Management and Outlook*. Second Edition. New York: John Wiley & Sons, 1980.

Dufey, G. "Banking in the Asia Pacific Area." Unpublished paper, University of Michigan, 1981.

Dufey, G. and Giddy, I. *The International Money Market*. Englewood Cliffs, N.J.: Prentice-Hall, Inc., 1978.

_____. "Innovation in the International Financial Markets," *Journal of International Business Studies* (Fall 1981), pp. 33-51.

Dunning, J. "The Determinants of International Production," *Oxford Economic Papers*, 25 (no. 3, 1973), pp. 289-336.

_____. "Trade, Location of Economic Activity and the MNE: A Search for an Eclectic Approach," in Ohlin, Hesselborn and Wijkman (eds.), *The International Allocation of Economic Activity*. New York: Holmes & Meier, 1977, pp. 395-418.

_____. "Explaining Changing Patterns of International Production: In Defence of the Eclectic Theory," *Oxford Bulletin of Economics and Statistics*, vol. 41 (November 1979), pp. 269-95.

_____. "Toward an Eclectic Theory of International Production: Some Empirical Tests," *Journal of International Business Studies* (Spring/Summer 1980), pp. 9-31.

_____. "Explaining the International Direct Investment Position of Countries: Towards a Dynamic or Developmental Approach," *Weltwirtschaftliches Archiv*, vol. 117, no. 1, 1981.

Fieleke, N. "The Growth of U.S. Banking Abroad: An Analytical Survey," in *Key Issues in International Banking*. Boston: Federal Reserve Bank of Boston, 1977.

Frowen, S. *A Framework of International Banking*. London: Guildford Educational Press, 1979.

Giddy, I. "The Theory of Industrial Organization of International Banking," in Hawkins, Levich and Wihlborg (eds.), *Internationalization of Financial Markets and National Economic Policy*. New York: JAI Press, 1981.

Goldberg, L. and Saunders, A. "The Causes of U.S. Bank Expansion Overseas," *Journal of Money, Credit and Banking* (November 1980), Part I.

_____. "The Growth of Organizatinal Forms of Foreign Banks in the United States," *Journal of Money, Credit and Banking*, 13 (August 1981), pp. 365-74.

_____. *Regulation and Foreign Market Growth by the International Banking Firm*. Working Paper Series No. 252 (February 1982). Salomon Brothers Center for the Study of Financial Institutions, Graduate School of Business Administration, New York University.

Goldberg, M. "The Direct Investment Decision of a Multinational Firm: With an Empirical Application to International Banking." Ph.D. dissertation, Northwestern University, 1973.

Gordon, R.A. "Issues in Multiple Regression," *The American Journal of Sociology*, 73 (1968), pp. 592-616.

Gray, J. and Gray, H. "The Multinational Bank: A Financial MNC?" *Journal of Banking and Finance*, 5 (1981), pp. 33-63.

Grubel, H. "A Theory of Multinational Banking," *Quarterly Review*, Banca Nazionale del Lavoro (December 1977), pp. 349-64.

Hanley, T. *United States Multinational Banking: Current and Prospective Strategies*. New York: Salomon Brothers, 1976.

Henning, C., Pigott, W. and Scott, R. *International Financial Management*. New York: McGraw-Hill Book Company, 1978.

Hodjera, Z. "The Asian Currency Market: Singapore as a Regional Financial Center." IMF Staff Paper (June 1978).

Horst, T. "Firm and Industry Determinants of the Decision to Invest Abroad: An Empirical Study," *The Review of Economics and Statistics*, 54 (August 1972).

Hultman, C.W. "Theories of International Commercial Banking Activity," *Rivista Internazionale di Scienze Economiche e Commerciali* (October-November 1980).

Hymer, S. *The International Operations of National Firms: A Study of Direct Foreign Investment*. Cambridge, Mass.: The MIT Press, 1976 (originally 1960).

Johnston, J. *Econometric Methods*. New York: McGraw-Hill Book Co., 1963.

Johnston, R. "International Banking, Risk, and U.S. Regulatory Policies," *Economic Review*, Federal Reserve Bank of San Francisco (Fall 1977).

Kelly, J. *Bankers and Borders: The Case of American Banks in Britain*. Cambridge, Mass.: Ballinger, 1977.

Khoury, S. *Dynamics of International Banking*. New York: Praeger Publishers, 1980.

Kindleberger, C.P. (ed.). *American Business Abroad: Six Lectures on Direct Investment*. New Haven, Conn.: Yale University Press, 1969.

_____. "The Formation of Financial Centers: A Study in Competitive Economic History," *Princeton Studies in International Finance*, no. 36, 1974.

Knickerbocker, F. *Oligopolistic Reaction and the Multinational Enterprise*. Boston, Mass.: Harvard University Press, 1973.

Korth, C. "The Evolving Role of U.S. Banks in International Finance," *The Bankers Magazine* (July-August 1981), pp. 68-73.

Kouzoul, J.P. "American Banks Abroad," in Kindleberger, C.P. (ed.), *The International Corporation: A Symposium.* Cambridge, Mass.: MIT Press, 1970.

LaPorte, P. and Young, A. "Clearing Asian Dollars through Singapore," *The Banker* (May 1981), pp. 149-53.

Lee, S.Y. *The Monetary and Banking Development of Malaysia and Singapore.* Singapore: Singapore University Press, 1974.

Lee, S.Y. and Jao, Y.C. *Financial Structures and Monetary Policies in Southeast Asia.* New York: St. Martin's Press, 1982.

Lees, F.A. *International Banking and Finance.* London and New York: MacMillan, 1974.

Little, J.S. "The Euro-dollar Market: Its Nature and Impact," *New England Economic Review*, Federal Reserve Bank of Boston (May-June 1969).

Monetary Authority of Singapore. *Financial Structure of Singapore.* Revised edition. Singapore, 1980.

Moore, G.S. "International Growth: Challenge to United States Banks," *The National Banking Review*, 1 (September 1963).

Mullineaux, D.J. "Economics of Scale and Organizational Efficiency in Banking; A Profit-function Approach," *Journal of Finance*, 33 (1978), pp. 259-80.

Odjagov, Marianne. "Foreign Ownership Policies of United States Multinational Banks," Ph.D. dissertation, Harvard University, 1978.

Officer, L. and Willett, T. "The Covered-Arbitrage Schedule: A Critical Survey of Recent Developments," *Journal of Money, Credit and Banking*, vol. 2, no. 2 (1970), pp. 244-55.

Osborn, N. "The Profit Squeeze Comes to International Banking," *Institutional Investor* (June 1981), pp. 239-55.

Pingle, R. "Why American Banks Go Overseas," *The Banker* (November 1966).

Porzecanski, A. "The International Financial Role of U.S. Commercial Banks: Past and Future," *Journal of Banking and Finance*, 5 (1981).

Prachowny, M.F.J. "A Note on Interest Parity and the Supply of Arbitrage Funds," *Journal of Political Economy*, vol. 78, no. 3 (1970), pp. 540-46.

Reed, E., Cotter, R., Gill, E. and Smith R. *Commercial Banking.* Englewood Cliffs, N.J.: Prentice-Hall, Inc., 1976.

Robinson, S., Jr. *Multinational Banking.* Leiden, Holland: A.W. Sijthoff International Publishing Company, 1972.

Rockefeller, D. *Creative Management in Banking.* New York: McGraw-Hill Book Company, 1964.

Rugman, A. "Internalization as a General Theory of Foreign Direct Investment: A Re-Appraisal of the Literature," *Weltwirtschaftliches Archiv*, 116 (no. 2, 1980), pp. 365-79.

_____. *Inside the Multinationals.* London: Croom Helm, 1981.

Stoll, H.R. "An Empirical Study of the Forward Exchange Market Under Fixed and Flexible Exchange Rate Systems," *Canadian Journal of Economics*, 1 (February 1968), pp. 55-78.

Tamaga, F. and Willis, P. "United States Banking Organization Abroad," *Federal Reserve Bulletin* (December 1956), pp. 1290-92.

Tan, C.H. *Financial Institutions in Singapore.* Singapore: Singapore University Press, 1981.

Terrell, H. and Key, S. "The U.S. Activities of Foreign Banks: An Analytic Survey." *International Finance Discussion Paper*, no. 113 (1977). Washington, D.C.: Board of Governors of the Federal Reserve System.

Thoman, G.R. "How to Serve the MNC Market." *The Banker* (August 1977).

Vastrup, C. "Economic Motives for Foreign Banking: The Danish Case," *Kredit and Kapital*, 1 (1983), pp. 117-25.

Von Clemm, M. "London Dollar CD: 10th Anniversary," *The Banker* (May 1976), pp. 607-9.

Wellons, P.A. *Transnational Banks*. Report to the Center on Transnational Corporations. New York: United Nations, 1976.

Williamson, O.E. *Markets and Hierarchies*. New York: Free Press, 1975.

Wong, Pakshong M. "The Asian Dollar Market Now," *Euromoney* (June 1975), pp. 100-102.

Yannopoulos, G. "Reasons for London's Dominance," *Built Environment*, 1 (1973), pp. 413-17.

_____. "The Growth of Transnational Banking," in Casson, M. (ed.), *The Growth of International Business*. London: George Allen and Unwin, 1983, pp. 236-57.

# Index